Second Workshop on Subword and Character Level Models in NLP 2018

New Orleans, Louisiana, USA
6 June 2018

ISBN: 978-1-5108-6361-3

NAACL HLT 2018

Subword and Character LEvel Models in NLP

Proceedings of the Second Workshop

June 6, 2018
New Orleans, Louisiana

Introduction

Traditional NLP starts with a hand-engineered layer of representation, the level of tokens or words. A tokenization component first breaks up the text into units using manually designed rules. Tokens are then processed by components such as word segmentation, morphological analysis and multiword recognition. The heterogeneity of these components makes it hard to create integrated models of both structure within tokens (e.g., morphology) and structure across multiple tokens (e.g., multi-word expressions). This approach can perform poorly (i) for morphologically rich languages, (ii) for noisy text, (iii) for languages in which the recognition of words is difficult and (iv) for adaptation to new domains; and (v) it can impede the optimization of preprocessing in end-to-end learning.

The workshop provides a forum for discussing recent advances as well as future directions on sub-word and character-level natural language processing and representation learning that address these problems.

Topics of Interest:

- tokenization-free models

- character-level machine translation

- character-ngram information retrieval

- transfer learning for character-level models

- models of within-token and cross-token structure

- NL generation (of words not seen in training etc)

- out of vocabulary words

- morphology and segmentation

- relationship b/w morphology and character-level models

- stemming and lemmatization

- inflection generation

- orthographic productivity

- form-meaning representations

- true end-to-end learning

- spelling correction

- efficient and scalable character-level models

Organizers

Organizers:

    Manaal Faruqui, Google
    Hinrich Schütze, LMU Munich
    Isabel Trancoso, INESC-ID/IST
    Yulia Tsvetkov, CMU
    Yadollah Yaghoobzadeh, MSR Montreal

Program Committee:

    Heike Adel, LMU Munich
    Rami Al-Rfou, Google
    Ehsan Asgari, UC Berkeley
    Miguel Ballesteros, IBM New York
    Gayatri Bhat, CMU
    Marta R. Costa-jussà, UPC Barcelona
    Ryan Cotterell, JHU
    Vera Demberg, Saarland
    Dan Garrette, Google
    Kevin Gimpel, TTIC
    Katharina Kann, LMU Munich
    Sachin Kumar, CMU
    Wang Ling, DeepMind
    Nanyun Peng, JHU
    Christopher Potts, Stanford
    Marek Rei, Cambridge
    Gaurav Singh Tomar, Google
    Eva Schlinger, Google
    Cicero dos Santos, IBM
    Laura Rimell, Google DeepMind
    Ngoc Thang Vu, Stuttgart
    Francois Yvon, LIMSI
    Alexander Rush, Harvard

Invited Speakers:

    Jacob Eisenstein, Georgia Tech
    Wang Ling, DeepMind
    Graham Neubig, CMU
    Barbara Plank, University of Groningen
    Brian Roark, Google

Table of Contents

Morphological Word Embeddings for Arabic Neural Machine Translation in Low-Resource Settings
Pamela Shapiro and Kevin Duh..1

Entropy-Based Subword Mining with an Application to Word Embeddings
Ahmed El-Kishky, Frank Xu, Aston Zhang, Stephen Macke and Jiawei Han..................12

A Comparison of Character Neural Language Model and Bootstrapping for Language Identification in Multilingual Noisy Texts
Wafia Adouane, Simon Dobnik, Jean-Philippe Bernardy and Nasredine Semmar..............22

Addressing Low-Resource Scenarios with Character-aware Embeddings
Sean Papay, Sebastian Padó and Ngoc Thang Vu...32

Subword-level Composition Functions for Learning Word Embeddings
Bofang Li, Aleksandr Drozd, Tao Liu and Xiaoyong Du...................................38

Discovering Phonesthemes with Sparse Regularization
Nelson F. Liu, Gina-Anne Levow and Noah A. Smith.....................................49

Meaningless yet meaningful: Morphology grounded subword-level NMT
Tamali Banerjee and Pushpak Bhattacharyya..55

Fast Query Expansion on an Accounting Corpus using Sub-Word Embeddings
Hrishikesh Ganu and Viswa Datha P..61

Incorporating Subword Information into Matrix Factorization Word Embeddings
Alexandre Salle and Aline Villavicencio..66

A Multi-Context Character Prediction Model for a Brain-Computer Interface
Shiran Dudy, Shaobin Xu, Steven Bedrick and David Smith..............................72

Conference Program

Wednesday, June 6, 2018

09:30–09:45   *Opening Remarks*
Manaal Faruqui

09:45–10:30   *Invited Talk: Orthographic Social Variation in Online Writing*
Jacob Eisenstein

10:30–11:00   ***Coffee Break***

11:00–11:45   *Invited Talk: Not All that Glitters is Gold*
Barbara Plank

11:45–12:00   ***Best paper talk 1. Sponsor: Microsoft Research***

12:00–14:00   ***Lunch Break***

14:00–14:45   *Invited Talk: Morphology – When is it Useful in Neural Models?*
Graham Neubig

14:45–15:45   **Poster Session and Coffee Break**

Morphological Word Embeddings for Arabic Neural Machine Translation in Low-Resource Settings
Pamela Shapiro and Kevin Duh

Entropy-Based Subword Mining with an Application to Word Embeddings
Ahmed El-Kishky, Frank Xu, Aston Zhang, Stephen Macke and Jiawei Han

A Comparison of Character Neural Language Model and Bootstrapping for Language Identification in Multilingual Noisy Texts
Wafia Adouane, Simon Dobnik, Jean-Philippe Bernardy and Nasredine Semmar

Addressing Low-Resource Scenarios with Character-aware Embeddings
Sean Papay, Sebastian Padó and Ngoc Thang Vu

Subword-level Composition Functions for Learning Word Embeddings
Bofang Li, Aleksandr Drozd, Tao Liu and Xiaoyong Du

Discovering Phonesthemes with Sparse Regularization
Nelson F. Liu, Gina-Anne Levow and Noah A. Smith

Meaningless yet meaningful: Morphology grounded subword-level NMT
Tamali Banerjee and Pushpak Bhattacharyya

Fast Query Expansion on an Accounting Corpus using Sub-Word Embeddings
Hrishikesh Ganu and Viswa Datha P

Incorporating Subword Information into Matrix Factorization Word Embeddings
Alexandre Salle and Aline Villavicencio

A Multi-Context Character Prediction Model for a Brain-Computer Interface
Shiran Dudy, Shaobin Xu, Steven Bedrick and David Smith

15:45–16:30   *Invited Talk: Romanization, Non-standard Orthography and Text Entry*
Brian Roark

16:30–16:45   ***Best paper talk 2. Sponsor: Microsoft Research***

16:45–17:30   *Invited Talk: What Makes a Character-level Neural Model work?*
Wang Ling

Morphological Word Embeddings for Arabic Neural Machine Translation in Low-Resource Settings

Pamela Shapiro
Johns Hopkins University
`pshapiro@jhu.edu`

Kevin Duh
Johns Hopkins University
`kevinduh@cs.jhu.edu`

Abstract

Neural machine translation has achieved impressive results in the last few years, but its success has been limited to settings with large amounts of parallel data. One way to improve NMT for lower-resource settings is to initialize a word-based NMT model with pretrained word embeddings. However, rare words still suffer from lower quality word embeddings when trained with standard word-level objectives. We introduce word embeddings that utilize morphological resources, and compare to purely unsupervised alternatives. We work with Arabic, a morphologically rich language with available linguistic resources, and perform Ar-to-En MT experiments on a small corpus of TED subtitles. We find that word embeddings utilizing subword information consistently outperform standard word embeddings on a word similarity task and as initialization of the source word embeddings in a low-resource NMT system.

1 Introduction

Neural machine translation (Bahdanau et al., 2014; Sutskever et al., 2014) has recently become the dominant approach to machine translation. However, the standard encoder-decoder models with attention have been shown to perform poorly in low-resource settings (Koehn and Knowles, 2017), a problem which can be alleviated by initialization of parameters from an NMT system trained on higher-resource languages (Zoph et al., 2016). An alternative way to initialize parameters in a low-resource NMT setup is to use pretrained monolingual word embeddings, which are quick to train and readily available for many languages.

There is a large body of work on word embeddings. Popular approaches include `word2vec` (Mikolov et al., 2013a) and `GloVe` (Pennington et al., 2014). These

have been shown to perform well in word similarity tasks and a variety of downstream tasks. However, they have been primarily evaluated on English. The learned representations for rare words are of low quality due to sparsity. For morphologically rich languages, we may want word embeddings that also consider morphological information, to reduce sparsity in word embedding training.

Previous work on morphological word embeddings has shown improvements on word similarity tasks, but has not been evaluated on downstream NMT tasks. Our contribution is two-fold:

1. We adapt `word2vec` to utilize lemmas from a morphological analyzer,[1] and show improvements on a word similarity task over a state-of-the-art unsupervised approach to incorporating morphological information based on character n-grams (Bojanowski et al., 2017).

2. We experiment with Arabic-to-English NMT on the TED Talks corpus. Our results demonstrate that incorporating some form of morphological word embeddings into NMT improves BLEU scores and outperforms the conventional approaches of using standard word embeddings, random initialization, or byte-pair encoding (BPE).

2 Neural Machine Translation

We follow recent work in neural machine translation, using a standard bi-directional LSTM encoder-decoder model with the attention mechanism from Luong et al. (2015). We describe below other work in NMT that has tried to address some of the same issues dealing with settings with limited parallel data, improving translation of morphological complexity, and Arabic NMT.

---

[1] `https://github.com/pamelashapiro/word2vec_morph`

1

Proceedings of the Second Workshop on Subword/Character LEvel Models, pages 1–11
New Orleans, Louisiana, June 6, 2018. ©2018 Association for Computational Linguistics

2.1 Low-Resource Settings

Some success has been achieved applying neural machine translation to low-resource settings. Zoph et al. (2016) use transfer learning to improve NMT from low-resource languages into English. They initialize parameters in the low-resource setting with parameters from an NMT model trained on a high-resource language. Nguyen and Chiang (2017) extend this by exploiting vocabulary overlap in related languages. Similarly, Firat et al. (2016) share parameters between high and low resource languages via multi-way, multilingual NMT.

Other work aims to exploit monolingual data via back-translation (Sennrich et al., 2016a). Imankulova et al. (2017) aim to improve this technique for low-resource settings by filtering generated back-translations with quality estimation. Meanwhile, He et al. (2016) use a reinforcement learning approach to learn from monolingual data.

Our approach is similar to those utilizing transfer learning, but we initialize on the source side with monolingual word embeddings, which is relatively simple to implement and low-cost to train. Di Gangi and Marcello (2017) experiment with monolingual word embeddings as we do, but they merge external monolingual word embeddings with the embeddings learned by an NMT system. We simply use word embeddings as initialization, and we instead focus on exploring how morphological word embeddings can help in this setup.

2.2 Incorporating Morphology

Some research has aimed to incorporate morphological information into NMT systems. Byte-Pair Encoding (BPE) segments words into pieces by merging character sequences based on frequency (Sennrich et al., 2016b), and these sequences of word pieces are translated. BPE become standard practice. However, it is unclear how much data is necessary for it to be beneficial. In our experiments, BPE performs worse than initializing with any of the word embeddings for our dataset.

Character-level NMT has recently become popular as well (Ling et al., 2015b; Costa-jussà and Fonollosa, 2016; Lee et al., 2017). Their work aims to implicitly learn morphology by building neural network architectures over characters. We also compare to a character-level NMT system in our experiments.

Additionally, Dalvi et al. (2017) add morphological information into the decoder, following work from Belinkov et al. (2017) that showed that the encoder already learns more morphological information than the decoder. Our work differs in that we are focusing on incorporating morphological information into the source side. Moreover, Belinkov et al. (2017) works with higher-resource datasets. It is possible that in lower-resource settings, it will still be helpful to incorporate morphological information into the encoder.

2.3 Arabic NMT

Almahairi et al. (2016) produce the first results of neural machine translation on Arabic. They find that preprocessing of Arabic as used in statistical machine translation is helpful. They normalize the text, removing diacritics and normalizing inconsistently typed characters, and they tokenize according the Penn Arabic Treebank (ATB) scheme (Maamouri et al., 2004), separating all clitics except for definite articles. We normalize as such, but do not use ATB tokenization, instead using the default tokenization in Moses (Koehn et al., 2007). We do this to focus on embeddings for words and to facilitate generalization to other languages. Additionally, Sajjad et al. (2017) explore alternatives to language-specific segmentation in Arabic, finding that BPE performs the best in their scenario.

Note that unlike the previously described work, we are using a dataset of only 2.9 million tokens for training. This is to assess the use of morphological word embeddings in settings with limited parallel data.

3 Morphological Word Embeddings

Morphological word embeddings help improve the quality of pretrained word embeddings for less frequent morphological variants, which is important for morphologically rich and low-resource languages. We outline related work in this section and describe an additional approach of our own.

Some related work has used morphological resources to guide word embeddings. Cotterell and Schütze (2015) use a multi-task objective to encourage word embeddings to reflect morphological tags, working within the log-bilinear model of Mnih and Hinton (2007). Cotterell et al. (2016) use a latent-variable model to adapt existing word embeddings to morphemes. Our additional approach is similar to this vein of work in that it uses morphological resources, but it works within the popu-

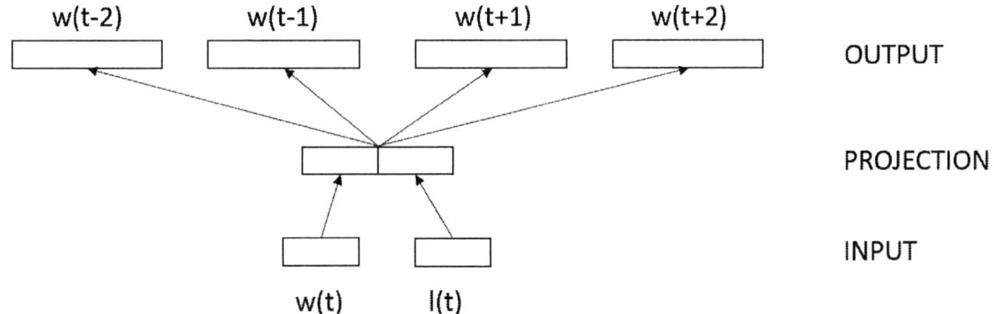

Figure 1: Modified skipgram objective for training `morph` embeddings. Here, w(t) is the current word, l(t) is its lemma, and w(t-2), w(t-1),w(t+1),w(t+2) are neighboring words.

lar `word2vec` skipgram objective (Mikolov et al., 2013a), adding a simple modification to consider a lemma in addition to a word form.

Other work uses purely unsupervised techniques. Luong et al. (2013) segment words using Morfessor (Creutz and Lagus, 2007), and use recursive neural networks to build word embeddings from morph embeddings. Instead of explicit segmentation, `fastText` (Bojanowski et al., 2017) incorporates subword information into the skipgram model by treating a word as a bag of character n-grams. They represent each n-gram of sizes 3-6 with a vector, and each word as a sum of its n-gram vectors. While `fastText` is not explicitly learning morphology, it can be viewed as potentially incorporating morpheme-like subwords.

For simplicity and efficiency, we consider only embeddings in the skipgram family—`fastText`, `word2vec` skipgram, and our modification of the `word2vec` skipgram objective, described in 3.1. There is a large literature on exploiting characters, morphology, and composition for embedding models (Chen et al., 2015; Ling et al., 2015a; Qiu et al., 2014; Wieting et al., 2016; Lazaridou et al., 2013), and a comparison with these different models may be interesting future work.

The usefulness of word embeddings in downstream applications is a question that often needs to be revisited. Many types of morphological or character-level embedding models have been evaluated under various extrinsic metrics, in applications such as language modeling (Kim et al., 2016; Botha and Blunsom, 2014; Sperr et al., 2013), parsing (Ballesteros et al., 2015), part-of-speech tagging (dos Santos and Zadrozny, 2014), and named-entity recognition (dos Santos and Guimarães, 2015; Cot-

terell and Duh, 2017). Besides the Arabic word similarity dataset, here we also focus on evaluating embeddings at the source side of a machine translation task.

3.1 Modified Skipgram Objective

We assume the availability of a morphological analyzer or lemmatizer that will output a lemma for each word token in a text. We modify the skipgram objective (Mikolov et al., 2013b) to use both word and lemma to predict context words, as illustrated in Figure 1. We learn word vectors and lemma vectors, using their concatenation in the dot product with a context vector in the skipgram objective. So the modified objective we are approximating with negative sampling is now

$$p(w_O|w_I, l_I) = \frac{\exp(v_{w_O}'^T \text{concat}(v_{w_I}, v_{l_I}))}{\sum_{w=1}^{W} \exp(v_w'^T \text{concat}(v_{w_I}, v_{l_I}))}$$

Without the lemma part, this objective corresponds to `word2vec`.

Because there may be multiple lemmas associated with a word type, we use a weighted average over lemma vectors in the final vector:

$$w_I^* = \text{concat}(\mathbf{v_{w_I}}, \frac{1}{c(w_I)} \sum_{l_I} c(w_I : l_I) * \mathbf{v_{l_I}})$$

where $c(\cdot)$ is the count of a word or word-lemma pair. When the morphological analyzer cannot produce a lemma, we use the word form itself. We output the vectors associated with individual lemmas as well, which can be used to handle OOV words.

The lemma simplifies a word, removing clitics and some inflectional morphology. While it reduces sparsity of infrequent stems, it also removes potentially useful information. The hope is that by using both word and lemma, we can maintain enough of the benefits of morphology in frequent words while also reducing sparsity in infrequent words. We do some preliminary experiments using just the lemma to predict context words as well, but in preliminary experiments this performed worse, possibly because we lose too much information from morphology.

In future work, we could also try modifying what is predicted as well (i.e. instead of predicting context words, predict lemma or both word and lemma).[2]

4 Arabic Morphology and Resources

We describe here the morphological analyzer we use, as well as prominent features of Arabic morphology that we consider in our analysis.

4.1 Morphological Analyzer

We use a morphological analyzer for Arabic called MADAMIRA (Pasha et al., 2014). MADAMIRA performs rule-based morphological analysis on the form of the word and then uses supervised learning techniques to disambiguate in context. It provides several types of morphological analysis for Arabic. In this work we only use the lemma, though future work could consider utilizing the other morphological information provided.

4.2 Arabic Morphology

One prominent feature of Arabic morphology is that it is rich with clitics, morphemes that syntactically function as words but phonologically function as affixes. Arabic proclitics (prefixes) include articles, conjunctions, and prepositions. Arabic enclitics (suffixes) include object or possessive pronouns. There are also inflectional affixes for number (singular, plural, and dual) and gender (masculine, feminine), and grammatical case endings - though only certain indefinite accusative case endings are visible without diacritics.

Semitic languages such as Arabic also have a substantial amount of non-concatenative morphology. Most stems are formed from a 3-consonant root inserted into a vowelled template, called "templatic morphology." When we are only considering inflectional morphology, as we are in the case of lemmas, we see this most in "broken plurals," which are especially productive in Arabic (as compared to other Semitic languages). A broken plural changes the internal vowelled pattern from the singular, rather than attaching a suffix.

An example of this is the word for "key," mftAH مفتاح, and its plural, mfAtyH مفاتيح, where the root is f-t-H, and the pattern for singular is mCCAC, and for plural is mCACyC.[3] In this case, MADAMIRA would produce the lemma: مفتاح_1 for both forms. We hypothesize that the embeddings informed by MADAMIRA will have an advantage on these words, where the morphemes involved cannot be captured by character n-grams.

5 Experiments

We compare three types of embeddings:

- `word2vec`: standard skip-gram word embeddings that only use word information.

- `fastText`: skip-gram embeddings that are sums of vectors representing character n-grams, implicitly incorporating some form of morphological information.

- `morph`: the modified skip-gram word embeddings described in Section 3.1, which rely on a morphological analyzer and lemma embeddings.

The word embeddings inserted into the NMT system are always of dimension 300, and in word similarity experiments, we experiment with dimensions of different sizes. All word embeddings are trained with negative sampling (5 samples), with a window size of 5, a 10^{-4} rejection threshold for subsampling, and 5 iterations. Additional `fastText` parameters are left at the default. We use OpenNMT-py (Klein et al., 2017) for all NMT experiments, with a max sentence size of 80. We use word-level prediction accuracy for model selection. For the BPE baseline, the number of BPE merge operations is 30,000. The hidden layer size is 1024, trained with batch size 80, with Adadelta (Zeiler, 2012) and a dropout rate of 0.2 for 20 epochs with a learning rate of 1.0.

When initializing the encoder with word embeddings, we experiment both with locking the word

---

[2]Our adaptation of `word2vec` can be used for context-dependent word tags in general, not just lemmas.

[3]We use Buckwalter transliteration (Buckwalter, 2002).

	Normalize Diacritics		Full Normalization	
	Null OOVs	**Handle OOVs**	**Null OOVs**	**Handle OOVs**
`word2vec`, 150	0.52	NA	0.52	NA
`word2vec`, 300	0.51	NA	0.53	NA
`fastText`, 150	0.53	0.55	0.55	0.55
`fastText`, 300	0.53	0.55	0.54	0.55
`morph`, 150-150, *word*	0.15	NA	0.15	NA
`morph`, 150-150, *word+lemma*	0.54	0.55	0.54	0.55
`morph`, 150-150, *lemma*	**0.59**	**0.60**	**0.59**	**0.60**

Table 1: Spearman coefficient for Arabic word similarity dataset built off of WS353. We list the dimension of the word embedding, and in the case of `morph`, we list the dimensions of the word part and the lemma part. In the `morph` system, *lemma* refers to using just the lemma part of the vector to compare similarity, *word* refers to using just the word part, and *word+lemma* refers to using the whole vector.

embeddings throughout training ("*fixed*") and allowing backpropagation through the word embeddings ("*unfixed*"). At test time, words not seen in the MT training data are also initialized with word embeddings, if they were seen in the word embedding training data. Words unseen by either corpus are mapped to the embedding of an `<unk>` token.

The bitext we use for NMT is a collection of TED subtitles obtained from WIT[3] (Cettolo et al., 2012).[4] This is a collection of monologue speeches from TED talks, covering a wide range of topics such technology, design, and social science. We downloaded the latest XML files (version 2016-04-08) for Arabic and performed subtitle extraction and sentence merging using the WIT[3] scripts. The data is then randomly split at the granularity of talks, with 1939 talks for training, 30 talks for development, and 30 talks for testing.[5] The corresponding sentence/token statistics are shown in Table 2. In this data, 9% of word types and 3% of tokens in the test data were not seen in train.

The monolingual corpus we use for word embeddings is cleaned and tokenized Arabic Wikipedia, consisting of about 80 million tokens, with a vocabulary of around 350k words. The word embeddings are trained on both the monolingual corpus and the source side of the TED training data. The number of lemma types in the monolingual corpus is 672k, and in TED training data is 42k.

5.1 Word Similarity Results

Before running NMT, we first experiment on a word similarity dataset to test the effectiveness of

Corpus	Sentences	Tokens	Types
Wikipedia	1,751k	79,793k	1,263k
TED, train	175k	2,855k	152k
TED, dev	2k	30k	8k
TED, test	2k	29k	8k

Table 2: Size of corpora, the number of tokens for MT data refers to the source side.

morphology in word embeddings. We compare `word2vec`, `fastText`, and variants of our morphological skip-gram in Section 3.1. We experiment with normalizing only diacritics as well as additionally normalizing inconsistently typed characters as in Almahairi et al. (2016), referred to here as "full normalization." We normalize the word similarity dataset accordingly. To ensure that dimensionality is not a major factor, we experiment with various dimensions. We also experiment with just using lemmas to predict, which performs slightly worse than using both word and lemma and taking the lemma part of the vector, though still better than `word2vec` and `fastText`.

We evaluate on an Arabic dataset developed by Hassan and Mihalcea (2009) based on the classic *WordSim353* (Finkelstein et al., 2001), as is evaluated on by Bojanowski et al. (2017). We re-run on `word2vec` and `fastText` and obtain similar, though not identical, results to Bojanowski et al. (2017). We suspect the differences are due to differences in cleaning and tokenizing Arabic Wikipedia. As is standard for these evaluations, we report Spearman rank coefficient in Table 1.

There are 3 OOV words when normalizing diacritics, and 1 with full normalization, out of 353

[4]`https://wit3.fbk.eu`
[5]The data splits are available at `http://www.cs.jhu.edu/~kevinduh/a/multitarget-tedtalks/`.

Model	Average	Δ	3 Runs
random initialization (word)	26.55	-	(26.40, 26.55, 26.70)
random initialization (BPE)	27.80	1.25	(27.64, 27.87, 27.90)
word2vec, *fixed*	26.97	0.42	(26.79, 27.00, 27.11)
word2vec, *unfixed*	28.38	1.83	(28.25, 28.38, 28.51)
morph, *fixed*	28.15	1.60	(27.91, 28.25, 28.29)
morph, *unfixed*	28.76	2.21	(28.50, 28.81, 28.96)
fastText, *fixed*	28.66	2.11	(28.62, 28.64, 28.71)
fastText, *unfixed*	**29.10**	2.55	(28.91, 29.15, 29.24)

Table 3: Corpus-level BLEU on the test set, averaged over 3 runs, with individual runs. Δ is the difference in BLEU between the model vs. random initialization with words as units.

Model	Average	Δ	3 Runs
random initialization (word)	22.85	-	(22.50, 22.90, 23.14)
word2vec, *unfixed*	24.89	2.04	(24.76, 24.96, 24.96)
morph, *unfixed*	25.49	2.64	(25.20, 25.42, 25.85)
fastText, *unfixed*	**25.77**	2.92	(25.49, 25.79, 26.02)

Table 4: BLEU on test sentences that have rare morphological variants. Δ is the difference in BLEU between the model vs. random initialization with words as units.

word pairs. We report results both using zero vectors for OOV and with an attempt to handle OOVs when possible, as done by Bojanowski et al. (2017). To handle OOVs, we run MADAMIRA on the unknown form alone (without the benefit of a context sentence) to get a lemma, and use the lemma vector learned for the corresponding lemma, if it was seen in training, with zeros for the word part.[6]

We see that across normalization schemes and dimensions, fastText performs 1-3 points better than word2vec in the null OOV setting and 2-4 points better handling OOVs. Using both word and lemma to predict context words performs about the same as fastText. However, when we take just the part of the vector corresponded to a weighted average of lemma vectors, it performs 4-6 points better than fastText. 2-4 points of this gain can be achieved by just using the lemma to predict context words.

Interestingly, the word part of the morph vector performs poorly on word similarity, but still provides some benefit in training. We found that using just the lemma to predict in training performed slightly worse than the lemma part of the vector when using both. It is possible that complementary features are learned in the word part and lemma part of the vector, and that the lemma part corresponds much more closely to semantic similarity.

5.2 Neural Machine Translation Results

We run 3 replicates of experiments with random initializations (re-training word embeddings on each run as well). Results for corpus-level BLEU, calculated using the multi_bleu.sh script from Moses are in provided in Table 3.

BPE outperforms using full words by 1.3 BLEU points (27.80 vs. 26.55). Initializing with word2vec results in a 1.8 BLEU point gain over randomly initialized word embeddings. morph results in a 0.4 BLEU point gain over word2vec, and fastText a 0.7 BLEU point gain. Fixing the embeddings consistently performs worse than allowing backpropagation. However, this gap narrows as the BLEU scores of both improve. We also compare to running a NMT system with a CNN over character embeddings in the encoder from Costa-jussà and Fonollosa (2016), which results in a BLEU score of 26.46. [7]

We also perform statistical significance testing via bootstrap resampling, using the multeval tool (Clark et al., 2011). The best BLEU are

---

[6] Note that when attempting to handle OOVs, in the case where we are only normalizing diacritics, we can only recover a lemma vector for 1 of the 3 OOVs while fastText is using n-grams to recover something for all 3. In the case of full normalization, both are able to recover a vector.

[7] We use the code from https://github.com/harvardnlp/seq2seq-attn, modifying hyperparameters to match our word-level models as closely as possible and using character-level default settings.

28.76 for `morph` and 29.10 for `fastText`. Both `morph` and `fastText` improve upon `word2vec` (28.38) with p-values < 0.01. The differences between `fastText` and `morph` are not statistically significant.

To see whether trends in BLEU are stronger for sentences containing rarer words with more frequent lemmas, we try filtering test sentences by the ratio of word count to lemma count in the source side of the MT training data. We take sentences with at least one word that has a lemma that is more than 50 times as frequent as the word in training data. Comparing just the unfixed, normalized, word-based versions, we show results for BLEU on filtered sentences in Table 4.

With this heuristic for rare morphological variants, there are 1,376 rare morphological variants out of the 7,345 words that are in the intersection of train and test source data. The heuristic pulls out 1,038 out of 1,982 test sentences to evaluate on. `morph` results in a 0.6 BLEU point gain over `word2vec`, and `fastText` a 0.88 BLEU point gain.

Because of corpus-level BLEU's limitations in characterizing translation quality with respect to morphological variants at the word level, we also perform a manual analysis of the sentences from each system to inspect improvements that may be due to the various word embeddings. We use `multeval` (Clark et al., 2011) to inspect the sentences that had the biggest sentence-level BLEU improvement over standard `word2vec` in the `morph` and `fastText` cases at the sentence level and see if there are notable trends. We display the median system's translation in this analysis, as recommended by Clark et al. (2011), though sentences selected here exhibited the phenomena described consistently across multiple runs. Example sentences are shown in Table 5.

In several cases, both `morph` and `fastText` systems consistently successfully translate rare or unseen words with morphological variants that are seen more commonly in the word embedding training data, while the `word2vec` system does not. For instance, in example 1, the word للتدخلات (*lltdxlAt*, "of interventions") is never seen in the MT training data. It is only seen rarely in the word embedding training data, 24 times. However, the word stripped of the definite article and the clitic corresponding to "of," i.e. the character n-gram تدخلات *tdxlAt*, is seen 657 times in word embed-

ding training data. The lemma, which is shared between singular and plural as well, occurs 6,887 times.

In some cases, the `morph` system is consistently the only system that successfully translates a rare morphological variant. For instance, in example 2, the `morph` system translates the word ابعادا (*AbEAdA*, "dimensions") correctly, while the other systems do not. It occurs here in the accusative case, which does not appear explicitly in many settings in Arabic. This word form occurs 7 times in the MT training data and 101 times in the monolingual corpus. Meanwhile, the lemma بُعد_1 occurs 214,297 times in the word embedding data. This is much more frequent than we'd expect to see variants of the word "dimension," because the lemma is also associated with the very frequent word for "after." However, it seems to learn a good representation despite this. It is unclear exactly why `fastText` does not learn a good representation in any of the three runs although it is possible that with character n-grams, there is conflict with other unrelated words. Note that because the plural is non-concatenative, none of the character n-grams in this word corresponds to the singular.

In other cases, the morphological analyzer cannot provide an analysis for a word, and a rare morphological variant is only translated correctly by `fastText`. In example 3, while sentence-level BLEU is best in the word2vec version in this case, we see a word that is translated best with `fastText`, and fails to be translated in the other two systems. The word ابتلاع (*AbtlAE*, "swallowing") is only seen as a word itself twice in MT training data and 171 times in the monolingual corpus. However, the 6-gram corresponding to the word is seen 444 times in the word embedding training data as a part of other words. Meanwhile, the morphological analyzer does not provide an analysis. While `fastText` translates as "swallow" rather than "swallowing," it is better than `morph` for this word, which consistently fails to translate the word at all.

6 Discussion

Overall, morphologically aware word embeddings (`morph` and `fastText`) can help reduce sparsity and improve results on both a word similarity task and a low-resource NMT system when used as initialization. The improvements over standard word embeddings is consistent, and implies that

src	و هكذا فتلك امثلة للتدخلات الايجابية. (1
src-Buckwalter	w hk*A ftlk Amvlp lltdxlAt AlAyjAbyp.
ref	So those are examples of positive interventions.
word2vec	And so these are examples of positive feedback.
morph	And so these are examples for positive interventions.
fastText	And so these are examples of positive interventions.
src	انا اخبركم ان هناك ابعادا كثيرة للتطور (2
src-Buckwalter	AnA Axbrkm An hnAk AbEAdA kvyrp lltTwr.
ref	I'm telling you that there are many dimensions of development.
word2vec	I'm telling you that there's a lot of implications of evolution.
morph	I'm telling you that there are many dimensions for evolution.
fastText	I'm telling you there's a lot of implications to evolution.
src	ابتلاع السيف هو من عادات الهند القديمة. (3
src-Buckwalter	AbtlAE Alsyf hw mn EAdAt Alhnd Alqdymp.
ref	Sword swallowing is from ancient India.
word2vec	The sword is a tradition of ancient India.
morph	The sword of the sword is a traditional Indian tradition.
fastText	Swallow the ball is the old Indian habits.

Table 5: Examples of sentences where word embeddings considering subword information are beneficial.

morphology is a useful signal to incorporate.

It is interesting that the word embeddings that perform best on a word similarity task (morph) do not line up with what performs best in an NMT system (fastText). This reinforces the argument that word similarity tasks alone are not enough to evaluate word embeddings (Faruqui et al., 2016), and that which embeddings we prefer may depend on the downstream task and the dataset. We discuss here briefly the potential strengths and weaknesses of each approach to morphological word embeddings, though more conclusive analysis is left to future work.

One possible reason for the difference in best embeddings between the two tasks, is how in-domain the morphological analyzer is for each task. In the word similarity task, 434 of the 444 unique words in the task receive lemmas (about 98%). On the other hand, in the MT test data, 7,266 out of 8,309 unique words receive lemmas (only about 87%).

It is also possible that function words matter more in the MT task, and that their translation does not improve as much with embeddings informed by lemmas. fastText may help more with these words, especially when function words in English correspond to pieces of a word in Arabic.

From these experiments, it appears that if one is more concerned with semantic similarity or has a dataset that lines up well with the morphological

analyzer used to produce lemmas, morphological word embeddings exploiting the morphological resources might be best. On the other hand, for a downstream task such as MT, and when there is a substantial number of words not covered by the analyzer, a method considering character n-grams may be better.

In both cases, word embeddings considering subword information consistently perform better than standard word embeddings on a morphologically rich language such as Arabic. It is possible that future gains could be made by combining the strengths of both models.

7 Conclusion

We extend the skipgram model for word embeddings to incorporate lemmas from a morphological resource in a simple way, maintaining the efficiency of word2vec, and release the code publicly. We show that this model outperforms word2vec and fastText on a word similarity task in Arabic.

We also conduct experiments with these word embeddings as initialization for a low-resource neural machine translation system. We find that the word embeddings utilizing subword information consistently outperform standard word embeddings at this task, and that any of the word embeddings we tried outperformed a random initialization or BPE. fastText does best at this task, with a 0.7

BLEU gain over standard word embeddings and 2.5 BLEU gain over random initialization.

Future work will attempt to combine the strengths of these multiple approaches to incorporating morphological information in word embeddings, as well as to explore other sources of information such as part-of-speech or syntax.

References

Amjad Almahairi, Kyunghyun Cho, Nizar Habash, and Aaron Courville. 2016. First result on arabic neural machine translation. *arXiv preprint arXiv:1606.02680* .

Dzmitry Bahdanau, Kyunghyun Cho, and Yoshua Bengio. 2014. Neural machine translation by jointly learning to align and translate. *arXiv preprint arXiv:1409.0473* .

Miguel Ballesteros, Chris Dyer, and Noah A. Smith. 2015. Improved transition-based parsing by modeling characters instead of words with lstms. In *Proceedings of the 2015 Conference on Empirical Methods in Natural Language Processing*. Association for Computational Linguistics, Lisbon, Portugal, pages 349–359. http://aclweb.org/anthology/D15-1041.

Yonatan Belinkov, Nadir Durrani, Fahim Dalvi, Hassan Sajjad, and James Glass. 2017. What do neural machine translation models learn about morphology? In *Proceedings of the 55th Annual Meeting of the Association for Computational Linguistics (Volume 1: Long Papers)*. Association for Computational Linguistics, pages 861–872. https://doi.org/10.18653/v1/P17-1080.

Piotr Bojanowski, Edouard Grave, Armand Joulin, and Tomas Mikolov. 2017. Enriching word vectors with subword information. *Transactions of the Association of Computational Linguistics* 5:135–146. http://www.aclweb.org/anthology/Q17-1010.

Jan Botha and Phil Blunsom. 2014. Compositional morphology for word representations and language modeling. In *Proceedings of the International Conference on Machine Learning (ICML)*.

Tim Buckwalter. 2002. Arabic transliteration. *URL http://www. qamus. org/transliteration. htm* .

Mauro Cettolo, Christian Girardi, and Marcello Federico. 2012. Wit^3: Web inventory of transcribed and translated talks. In *Proceedings of the 16th Conference of the European Association for Machine Translation (EAMT)*. Trento, Italy, pages 261–268.

Xinxiong Chen, Lei Xu, Zhiyuan Liu, Maosong Sun, and Huanbo Luan. 2015. Joint learning of character and word embeddings. https://www.aaai.org/ocs/index.php/IJCAI/IJCAI15/paper/view/11000.

Jonathan H. Clark, Chris Dyer, Alon Lavie, and Noah A. Smith. 2011. Better hypothesis testing for statistical machine translation: Controlling for optimizer instability. In *Proceedings of the 49th Annual Meeting of the Association for Computational Linguistics: Human Language Technologies*. Association for Computational Linguistics, pages 176–181. http://www.aclweb.org/anthology/P11-2031.

Marta R. Costa-jussà and José A. R. Fonollosa. 2016. Character-based neural machine translation. In *Proceedings of the 54th Annual Meeting of the Association for Computational Linguistics (Volume 2: Short Papers)*. Association for Computational Linguistics, pages 357–361. https://doi.org/10.18653/v1/P16-2058.

Ryan Cotterell and Kevin Duh. 2017. Low-resource named entity recognition with cross-lingual, character-level neural conditional random fields. In *Proceedings of the Eighth International Joint Conference on Natural Language Processing (Volume 2: Short Papers)*. Asian Federation of Natural Language Processing, Taipei, Taiwan, pages 91–96. http://www.aclweb.org/anthology/I17-2016.

Ryan Cotterell and Hinrich Schütze. 2015. Morphological word-embeddings. In *Proceedings of the 2015 Conference of the North American Chapter of the Association for Computational Linguistics: Human Language Technologies*. Association for Computational Linguistics, pages 1287–1292. https://doi.org/10.3115/v1/N15-1140.

Ryan Cotterell, Hinrich Schütze, and Jason Eisner. 2016. Morphological smoothing and extrapolation of word embeddings. In *Proceedings of the 54th Annual Meeting of the Association for Computational Linguistics (Volume 1: Long Papers)*. Association for Computational Linguistics, pages 1651–1660. https://doi.org/10.18653/v1/P16-1156.

Mathias Creutz and Krista Lagus. 2007. Unsupervised models for morpheme segmentation and morphology learning. *ACM Transactions on Speech and Language Processing (TSLP)* 4(1):3.

Fahim Dalvi, Nadir Durrani, Hassan Sajjad, Yonatan Belinkov, and Stephan Vogel. 2017. Understanding and improving morphological learning in the neural machine translation decoder. In *Proceedings of the Eighth International Joint Conference on Natural Language Processing (Volume 1: Long Papers)*. volume 1, pages 142–151.

Mattia A Di Gangi and Federico Marcello. 2017. Can monolingual embeddings improve neural machine translation? .

Cicero dos Santos and Victor Guimarães. 2015. Boosting named entity recognition with neural character embeddings. In *Proceedings of the Fifth Named Entity Workshop*. Association for Computational Linguistics, Beijing, China, pages 25–33. http://www.aclweb.org/anthology/W15-3904.

Cicero Nogueira dos Santos and Bianca Zadrozny. 2014. Learning character-level representations for part-of-speech tagging. In *ICML*.

Manaal Faruqui, Yulia Tsvetkov, Pushpendre Rastogi, and Chris Dyer. 2016. Problems with evaluation of word embeddings using word similarity tasks. https://doi.org/10.18653/v1/W16-2506.

Lev Finkelstein, Evgeniy Gabrilovich, Yossi Matias, Ehud Rivlin, Zach Solan, Gadi Wolfman, and Eytan Ruppin. 2001. Placing search in context: The concept revisited. In *Proceedings of the 10th international conference on World Wide Web*. ACM, pages 406–414.

Orhan Firat, Kyunghyun Cho, and Yoshua Bengio. 2016. Multi-way, multilingual neural machine translation with a shared attention mechanism. In *Proceedings of the 2016 Conference of the North American Chapter of the Association for Computational Linguistics: Human Language Technologies*. Association for Computational Linguistics, pages 866–875. https://doi.org/10.18653/v1/N16-1101.

Samer Hassan and Rada Mihalcea. 2009. Cross-lingual semantic relatedness using encyclopedic knowledge. In *Proceedings of the 2009 Conference on Empirical Methods in Natural Language Processing*. Association for Computational Linguistics, pages 1192–1201. http://www.aclweb.org/anthology/D09-1124.

Di He, Yingce Xia, Tao Qin, Liwei Wang, Nenghai Yu, Tieyan Liu, and Wei-Ying Ma. 2016. Dual learning for machine translation. In *Advances in Neural Information Processing Systems*. pages 820–828.

Aizhan Imankulova, Takayuki Sato, and Mamoru Komachi. 2017. Improving low-resource neural machine translation with filtered pseudo-parallel corpus. In *Proceedings of the 4th Workshop on Asian Translation (WAT2017)*. Asian Federation of Natural Language Processing, Taipei, Taiwan, pages 70–78. http://www.aclweb.org/anthology/W17-5704.

Yoon Kim, Yacine Jernite, David Sontag, and Alexander M Rush. 2016. Character-aware neural language models. In *AAAI*. pages 2741–2749.

Guillaume Klein, Yoon Kim, Yuntian Deng, Jean Senellart, and Alexander Rush. 2017. Opennmt: Open-source toolkit for neural machine translation. In *Proceedings of ACL 2017, System Demonstrations*. Association for Computational Linguistics, pages 67–72. http://www.aclweb.org/anthology/P17-4012.

Philipp Koehn, Hieu Hoang, Alexandra Birch, Chris Callison-Burch, Marcello Federico, Nicola Bertoldi, Brooke Cowan, Wade Shen, Christine Moran, Richard Zens, Chris Dyer, Ondrej Bojar, Alexandra Constantin, and Evan Herbst. 2007. Moses: Open source toolkit for statistical machine translation. In *Proceedings of the 45th Annual Meeting of the Association for Computational Linguistics Companion Volume Proceedings of the Demo and Poster Sessions*. Association for Computational Linguistics, pages 177–180. http://www.aclweb.org/anthology/P07-2045.

Philipp Koehn and Rebecca Knowles. 2017. Six challenges for neural machine translation. In *Proceedings of the First Workshop on Neural Machine Translation*. Association for Computational Linguistics, Vancouver, pages 28–39. http://www.aclweb.org/anthology/W17-3204.

Angeliki Lazaridou, Marco Marelli, Roberto Zamparelli, and Marco Baroni. 2013. Compositional-ly derived representations of morphologically complex words in distributional semantics. In *Proceedings of the 51st Annual Meeting of the Association for Computational Linguistics (Volume 1: Long Papers)*. Association for Computational Linguistics, Sofia, Bulgaria, pages 1517–1526. http://www.aclweb.org/anthology/P13-1149.

Jason Lee, Kyunghyun Cho, and Thomas Hofmann. 2017. Fully character-level neural machine translation without explicit segmentation. *Transactions of the Association for Computational Linguistics* 5:365–378. https://transacl.org/ojs/index.php/tacl/article/view/1051.

Wang Ling, Chris Dyer, Alan W Black, Isabel Trancoso, Ramon Fermandez, Silvio Amir, Luis Marujo, and Tiago Luis. 2015a. Finding function in form: Compositional character models for open vocabulary word representation. In *Proceedings of the 2015 Conference on Empirical Methods in Natural Language Processing*. Association for Computational Linguistics, Lisbon, Portugal, pages 1520–1530. http://aclweb.org/anthology/D15-1176.

Wang Ling, Isabel Trancoso, Chris Dyer, and Alan W Black. 2015b. Character-based neural machine translation. *arXiv preprint arXiv:1511.04586*.

Thang Luong, Hieu Pham, and Christopher D. Manning. 2015. Effective approaches to attention-based neural machine translation. In *Proceedings of the 2015 Conference on Empirical Methods in Natural Language Processing*. Association for Computational Linguistics, pages 1412–1421. https://doi.org/10.18653/v1/D15-1166.

Thang Luong, Richard Socher, and Christopher Manning. 2013. Better word representations with recursive neural networks for morphology. http://www.aclweb.org/anthology/W13-3512.

Mohamed Maamouri, Ann Bies, Tim Buckwalter, and Wigdan Mekki. 2004. The penn arabic treebank: Building a large-scale annotated arabic corpus. In *NEMLAR conference on Arabic language resources and tools*. volume 27, pages 466–467.

Tomas Mikolov, Kai Chen, Greg Corrado, and Jeffrey Dean. 2013a. Efficient estimation of word representations in vector space. *arXiv preprint arXiv:1301.3781* .

Tomas Mikolov, Ilya Sutskever, Kai Chen, Greg S Corrado, and Jeff Dean. 2013b. Distributed representations of words and phrases and their compositionality. In *Advances in neural information processing systems*. pages 3111–3119.

Andriy Mnih and Geoffrey Hinton. 2007. Three new graphical models for statistical language modelling. In *Proceedings of the 24th international conference on Machine learning*. ACM, pages 641–648.

Toan Q. Nguyen and David Chiang. 2017. Transfer learning across low-resource, related languages for neural machine translation. In *Proceedings of the Eighth International Joint Conference on Natural Language Processing (Volume 2: Short Papers)*. Asian Federation of Natural Language Processing, Taipei, Taiwan, pages 296–301. http://www.aclweb.org/anthology/I17-2050.

Arfath Pasha, Mohamed Al-Badrashiny, Mona Diab, Ahmed El Kholy, Ramy Eskander, Nizar Habash, Manoj Pooleery, Owen Rambow, and Ryan Roth. 2014. Madamira: A fast, comprehensive tool for morphological analysis and disambiguation of arabic. In *Proceedings of the Ninth International Conference on Language Resources and Evaluation (LREC-2014)*. European Language Resources Association (ELRA). http://www.aclweb.org/anthology/L14-1479.

Jeffrey Pennington, Richard Socher, and Christopher Manning. 2014. Glove: Global vectors for word representation. In *Proceedings of the 2014 Conference on Empirical Methods in Natural Language Processing (EMNLP)*. Association for Computational Linguistics, pages 1532–1543. https://doi.org/10.3115/v1/D14-1162.

Siyu Qiu, Qing Cui, Jiang Bian, Bin Gao, and Tie-Yan Liu. 2014. Co-learning of word representations and morpheme representations. In *Proceedings of COLING 2014, the 25th International Conference on Computational Linguistics: Technical Papers*. Dublin City University and Association for Computational Linguistics, Dublin, Ireland, pages 141–150. http://www.aclweb.org/anthology/C14-1015.

Hassan Sajjad, Fahim Dalvi, Nadir Durrani, Ahmed Abdelali, Yonatan Belinkov, and Stephan Vogel. 2017. Challenging language-dependent segmentation for arabic: An application to machine translation and part-of-speech tagging. In *Proceedings of the 55th Annual Meeting of the Association for Computational Linguistics (Volume 2: Short Papers)*. Association for Computational Linguistics, pages 601–607. https://doi.org/10.18653/v1/P17-2095.

Rico Sennrich, Barry Haddow, and Alexandra Birch. 2016a. Improving neural machine translation models with monolingual data. In *Proceedings of the 54th Annual Meeting of the Association for Computational Linguistics (Volume 1: Long Papers)*. Association for Computational Linguistics, pages 86–96. https://doi.org/10.18653/v1/P16-1009.

Rico Sennrich, Barry Haddow, and Alexandra Birch. 2016b. Neural machine translation of rare words with subword units. In *Proceedings of the 54th Annual Meeting of the Association for Computational Linguistics (Volume 1: Long Papers)*. Association for Computational Linguistics, pages 1715–1725. https://doi.org/10.18653/v1/P16-1162.

Henning Sperr, Jan Niehues, and Alex Waibel. 2013. Letter n-gram-based input encoding for continuous space language models. In *Proceedings of the Workshop on Continuous Vector Space Models and their Compositionality*. Association for Computational Linguistics, Sofia, Bulgaria, pages 30–39. http://www.aclweb.org/anthology/W13-3204.

Ilya Sutskever, Oriol Vinyals, and Quoc V Le. 2014. Sequence to sequence learning with neural networks. In *Advances in neural information processing systems*. pages 3104–3112.

John Wieting, Mohit Bansal, Kevin Gimpel, and Karen Livescu. 2016. Charagram: Embedding words and sentences via character n-grams. In *Proceedings of the 2016 Conference on Empirical Methods in Natural Language Processing*. Association for Computational Linguistics, Austin, Texas, pages 1504–1515. https://aclweb.org/anthology/D16-1157.

Matthew D Zeiler. 2012. Adadelta: an adaptive learning rate method. *arXiv preprint arXiv:1212.5701* .

Barret Zoph, Deniz Yuret, Jonathan May, and Kevin Knight. 2016. Transfer learning for low-resource neural machine translation. In *Proceedings of the 2016 Conference on Empirical Methods in Natural Language Processing*. Association for Computational Linguistics, pages 1568–1575. https://doi.org/10.18653/v1/D16-1163.

Entropy-Based Subword Mining with an Application to Word Embeddings

Ahmed El-Kishky[1]**, Frank Xu**[2]**, Aston Zhang**[3]**, Stephen Macke**[1]**, Jiawei Han**[1]
The University of Illinois at Urbana Champaign
Shanghai Jiao Tong University
Amazon Inc.
{elkishk2,smacke, hanj}@illinois.edu[1], frankxu@sjtu.edu.cn[2], astonz@amazon.com[3]

Abstract

Recent literature has shown a wide variety of benefits to mapping traditional one-hot representations of words and phrases to lower-dimensional real-valued vectors known as word embeddings. Traditionally, most word embedding algorithms treat each word as the finest meaningful semantic granularity and perform embedding by learning distinct embedding vectors for each word. Contrary to this line of thought, technical domains such as scientific and medical literature compose words from subword structures such as prefixes, suffixes, and root-words as well as compound words. Treating individual words as the finest-granularity unit discards meaningful shared semantic structure between words sharing substructures. This not only leads to poor embeddings for text corpora that have long-tail distributions, but also heuristic methods for handling out-of-vocabulary words. In this paper we propose SubwordMine, an entropy-based subword mining algorithm that is fast, unsupervised, and fully data-driven. We show that this allows for great cross-domain performance in identifying semantically meaningful subwords. We then investigate utilizing the mined subwords within the FastText embedding model and compare performance of the learned representations in a downstream language modeling task.

1   Introduction

In recent years, distributed continuous word representations have become a popular tool for providing a low-dimensional, alternative representation to traditional one-hot bag of words (Rumelhart et al., 1988; Elman, 1990). These word-embedding vectors are typically a real-valued vector of dimensionality much smaller than the vocabulary size of a corpus. In addition to computational efficiency of working with low-dimensional representations, distributed representations have

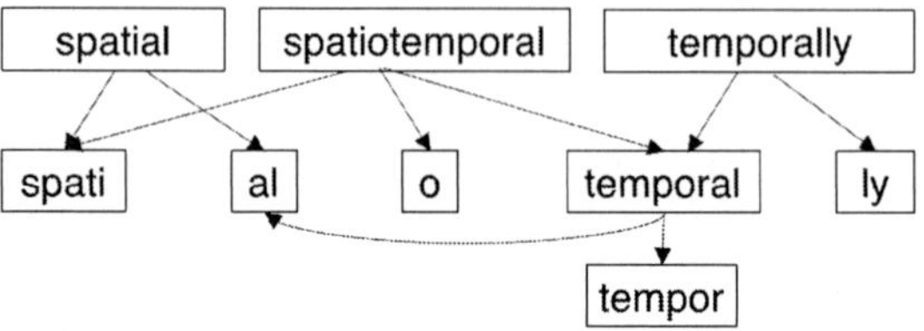

Figure 1: Hierarchical segmentation of words *spatial, spatiotemporal, temporally* into subwords.

been shown to capture syntactic and semantic regularities and have been shown to boost the performance in tasks such as text classification, sequential classification, sentiment analysis, and machine translation (Mikolov et al., 2013c; Joulin et al., 2017; Huang et al., 2015; Tang et al., 2014; Zou et al., 2013). Many different methods have been proposed to derive these continuous representations from large, unlabeled, text corpora (Collobert and Weston, 2008; Mikolov et al., 2013a,b).

While distributed continuous representations have helped push the state-of-the-art in a variety of NLP tasks, because most text corpora have long-tail distributions, embeddings in the long-tail are often of poor quality due to infrequency. This is even worse for out-of-vocabulary words which are all given the same constant embedding vector because no information is available to infer a meaningful representation. To address this deficiency, we propose to mine smaller subword structures that form the base syntactic unit and leverage the discovered subwords for generating better-quality word embeddings. As seen in Figure 1, morphologically-rich words often contain semantically meaningful subwords that are shared among many words. Understanding the semantic meaning of these subwords can be used to infer the meaning of words that contain them. With this motivation, we propose SubwordMine,

Proceedings of the Second Workshop on Subword/Character LEvel Models, pages 12–21
New Orleans, Louisiana, June 6, 2018. ©2018 Association for Computational Linguistics

an algorithm for mining semantically-meaningful subwords from corpus vocabulary. We utilize the mined subwords as the base-unit for embedding and combine them to construct a word's distributed vector representation. The resultant word embeddings are robust to data-sparsity due to word infrequency and can be constructed on many out-of-vocabulary words.

We state and analyze the problem in Section 2, followed by our proposed solution in Section 3 where we present the key components of our solution, subword mining and subword-based word embeddings. In Section 4, we review the related work. Then we evaluate the proposed solution in Section 5, conclude in Section 6, and present future directions in Section 7.

2 SubwordMine Framework

We formalize and analyze the task of extracting subword structure and propose a framework for entropy-based subword mining.

2.1 Preliminaries

The input is a corpus W, consisting of $|W|$ words: $W = w_1, \ldots, w_{|W|}$. From this corpus, we construct a vocabulary of unique words, V, of size $|V|$ such that $\forall w \in W, w \in V$. In addition, the v_{th} word is a sequence of $|v|$ characters: $c_{v,i}, i = 1, \ldots, |v|$. For convenience we index all the unique characters that compose the input vocabulary with C characters and $c_{v,i} = x, x \in \{1, \ldots, C\}$ means that the i_{th} character in v_{th} word is the x_{th} character in the character vocabulary. Given an input corpus consisting of a word sequence and a vocabulary list of unique words, our goal is to segment the vocabulary list to identify human-interpretable and semantically meaningful subwords, then utilize these subwords for parameter sharing when learning distributed word representations from the corpus.

Definition 1 (Subword Formalization) *We formally define subwords and other necessary notation and terminology as follows:*

- *A subword is a sequence of contiguous characters:* $s = \{c_{v,i}, \ldots c_{v,i+n}\}\ n > 0$

- *A partition over v_{th} word is a sequence of subwords:* $\mathcal{G}_v = (s_{v,1}, \ldots, s_{v,G_v})\ G_v \geq 1$ *s.t. the concatenation of the subword instances is the original word.*

In Definition 1 we formalize a subword and the resultant partition from segmenting a vocabulary word into subwords. In addition we outline the desired properties of the resultant subword as well as the mining and embedding framework as follows:

- The subwords extracted are semantically-meaningful and human-interpretable.

- Utilizing these subwords improves word embeddings.

- The overall method is computationally efficient.

- The number of subwords generated is comparable to the vocabulary size.

2.2 SubwordMine Framework

To extract subwords that satisfy our desired requirements, we propose a framework that can be divided into two sequential steps: 1) subword pattern mining 2) subword segmentation. Our process for transforming each word in the input vocabulary word to a high-quality 'bag-of-subwords' involves creating a subword vocabulary, and then using these subwords to hierarchically segment each word in the vocabulary. By applying an information-theoretic metric to detect candidate subword boundaries, we identify candidate subwords within each vocabulary word. From this candidate pool, we then apply an unsupervised dynamic programming segmentation algorithm to select a subset of these subwords that best segment the word. After inducing a partition on each word, we can recursively segment each subword to an arbitrary level of subword granularity. The resultant subwords from the hierarchical segmentation can then be used for word embedding.

The goal of frequent subword pattern mining is to collect aggregate statistics on subword patterns for use in the word segmentation algorithm. For each character-ngram that appears more than once in the vocabulary, there is the potential for parameter sharing via that candidate subword. Additionally the frequency counts of these subwords will be used for entropy-boundary computation to identify potential subword candidates. These candidates are inputted to the word-segmentation algorithm that attempts to apply Occam's Razor by selecting subwords that maximally cover each word using the fewest number of subwords. Each subword can then be recursively segmented into further subwords.

3 Methodology

We present a subword mining algorithm that, given an input vocabulary list V, segments each vocabulary word into, non-overlapping, character-ngrams. Our method is purely data-driven relying on character co-occurence statistics allowing for good cross-domain performance on a variety of scientific datasets. Additionally the method operates directly on an input vocabulary list, forgoing any corpus-level statistics. This allows for more scalable subword extraction as passes over large corpora are unnecessary. From a high-level perspective, the subword segmentation algorithm can be decomposed into the following steps:

1. Mine candidate subword counts and compute relevant co-occurence statistics.

2. Apply SubwordMine to segment each word.

3. Recurse for finer-grained subword segmentation.

We apply an entropy-based scoring function to identify subword boundaries: generating candidate subwords. Given a collection of subwords, the next step in the framework is to apply a dynamic-programming algorithm to segment each word into subwords. The framework proceeds to recursively segment each subword in the segmentation. We will discuss these steps in greater detail in the next subsections.

3.1 Subword Vocabulary Generation

Our segmentation of words into subwords relies on the idea of subword compositionality. That is, the input vocabulary can be constructed by composing subwords drawn from a smaller subword vocabulary. As such we introduce a two-step approach for creating the initial subword vocabulary: prefix and suffix generation followed by root-word generation.

Prefix & Suffix Generation

The first step in creating the subword vocabulary is to generate a set of high-quality prefixes and suffixes. The method is based on the principle that a high-quality prefix or suffix can be measured by a high level of unpredictability in transition to longer substrings from the current substring state. For example, following the prefix "pr", most prefixes transition to the character "e" with high probability forming a prefix "pre". On the other

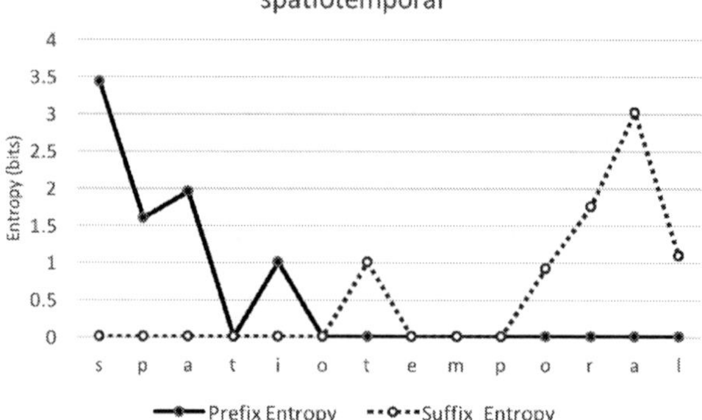

Figure 2: Entropy for candidate prefixes and suffixes in the word "spatiotemporal" from a DBLP titles dataset.

hand, transitioning from "pre" to a longer prefix is not as predictable as a large number of words contain the prefix "pre" followed by a variety of root words starting with different characters. We identify these high-unpredictability boundaries using the concept of information entropy to score the predictability of each prefix or suffix boundary (Shannon, 2001).

Let v be a word consisting of $|v|$ characters and s_i be a prefix of w ending at the i_{th} character of w. For each candidate prefix boundary i for $i \in [1 \ldots |v|]$, the information entropy of the prefix is computed as follows:

$$\mathcal{E}(i) = -\sum_{j=1}^{C} \mathrm{P}(s_i \oplus c_j | s_i) \times \log_2 \mathrm{P}(s_i \oplus c_j | s_i)$$

(1)

Where $\oplus$ denotes the binary concatenation of two subwords and the transitional probabilities between a prefix and the prefix with the next character appended is estimated by:

$$\mathrm{P}(s_i \oplus c_j | s_i) = \frac{f(s_i \oplus c_j)}{f(s_i)}$$

(2)

and $f(s_i)$ denotes the frequency of a prefix s_i in the input vocabulary list. The entropy of suffixes can, without loss of generality, be similarly computed by reversing each word in the vocabulary and treating each suffix as a prefix.

The information entropy of each possible prefix and suffix in the vocabulary is computed in linear time using a prefix tree data structure to store counts over prefixes. Given entropy scores for each prefix and suffix, scores are computed for each candidate split point in each word. Under the entropy scoring of prefixes and suffixes, we identify *local maxima* in entropy as candidate boundaries for prefixes and suffixes. That is entropy of prefixes of one-character shorter and one-character longer should be lower than a candidate prefix boundary. This is intuitive as under our principle of compositionality assumption, complex words are formed by concatenating subword structures. As such, given an incomplete subword, the next character can easily be predicted, but given a complete subword, any number of new subwords can be concatenated to the completed subword increasing the unpredictability and thus entropy. These high-entropy positions thus serve as a strong indicator of subword boundaries. As seen in Figure 2, for the word "spatiotemporal", candidate prefixes and suffixes are found at boundaries exhibit a local maxima in entropy. For "spatiotemporal", candidate prefixes are "spa" and "spati" while candidate suffixes include "al" and "temporal".

Root Word Generation

While utilizing entropy-scoring, it is possible to detect subword structures that occur at the beginning or end of a word, often many words contain subword structure between prefixes and suffixes. For each prefix and suffix candidate identified in a word, it is possible to generate candidate root word by stemming the word and removing prefixes and suffixes. This creates a high-quality pool of rootwords to be used in conjunction with prefixes and suffixes for segmenting the vocabulary.

Example 1 (Root Extraction) *Removing prefixes and suffixes yields candidate root words.*

$$[pre] + \underline{authenticat} + [ion]$$

The characters grouped together by [] are prefixes and suffixes. When removed, the remaining underlined character-sequence represent candidate root words.

As seen in Example 1, when stripping the possible prefixes and suffixes of a word, the remaining character sequence is considered a candidate root word. We apply some filtering conditions for each candidate root to test the viability as a shareable root. These include: 1) a minimum support of two within the vocabulary 2) the entropy boundary of each rootword must be non-zero. Additionally, for each word in the vocabulary, after stripping prefixes and suffixes, the candidate root words that meet the root word constraints are extracted and added to the subword vocabulary.

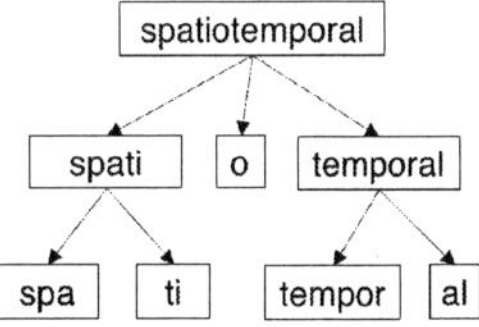

(a) Parsimonious Segmentation (b) Candidate Subwords

Figure 3: Segmentation of the word "spatiotemporal" using disjoint interval covering.

3.2 Parsimonious Subword Segmentation

In the previous section, we introduce an unsupervised method of subword generation based on an entropy-based predictability metric for boundary detection. In this subsection we introduce an unsupervised segmentation algorithm that, utilizing a given subword vocabulary, segments a word into subwords. Our algorithm first identifies candidate subwords from the subword vocabulary within a word, then selects a subset of these candidate subwords that best segment the word. The main insight behind the unsupervised segmentation is a per-word implementation of Occam's Razor. That is, according to the preference for parsimonious hypotheses, we posit that each word is composed of the *fewest number of subwords that maximally cover the word*.

Example 2 (Parsimonious Segmentation) *According to parsimonious segmentation, candidate segmentations are scored based on word coverage and number of subwords used for coverage.*

Segmentation	# Subwords	Coverage
[spa] + tio+ [temporal]	2	11
[spati] + o + [temporal]	2	13
[spati] + o + [tempor] + [al]	3	13
...		
[spa] + tio [tempor] + [al]	3	11

The highlighted row displays the maximally parsimonious subword segmentation.

As seen in Figure 3, for each word a set of subwords present in the target word are identified and recursive segmentation is performed to separate the word into subwords. Example 2 demonstrates how the candidates are used to segment the target word under the *parsimony criterion*. Subsets of non-overlapping candidate subwords are used to segment and the most parsimonious segmentation is selected. Because there are a $\mathcal{O}(2^{|A_v|})$ number of possible subsets of candidate subwords, direct enumeration of each segmentation quickly proves intractable for even a modest number of candidate subwords. To identify the most parsimonious seg-

15

mentation, we abstract out our parsimonious subword segmentation task into a general problem we dub *Disjoint Interval Covering* and demonstrate that this problem can be solved via dynamic programming in linear time.

We formalize the disjoint interval covering problem as follows:

Definition 2 (Disjoint Interval Covering)
Given an input $N \in \mathbb{N}$ and a set A of pairs $(a, b) : a, b \in \{1 \ldots N\} \times \{1 \ldots N\}$ and $a < b$, find the smallest subset $B \subseteq A$ such that $|\bigcup_{x \in B} x|$ is maximized, $|B|$ is minimized, and $\forall x, y \in B : x \neq y \Rightarrow x \cap y = \varnothing$.

As seen in Definition 2, the input is a set of pairs A and a positive integer N. Within the segmentation perspective, these refer to position index boundary pairs for candidate subwords and the word length. Given these inputs, the objective is to select a minimum subset of disjoint subwords whose length maximize coverage of the word.

$$F(j) = \max_{0} \min_{1} \begin{cases} (0,0), & j < 1 \\ F(j-1), & j \geq 1 \\ \max_{0} \min_{1}_{(i,j) \in B} \{F(i-1)_0 + (j-i+1), F(i-1)_1+1\}, & j \geq 1 \end{cases} \tag{3}$$

We define a recurrence to the disjoint interval covering problem in Equation 3. This recurrence posits that the segmentation that maximally covers the word is either the solution for the current word minus the ending character, or the max-covering, min-subword solution utilizing all subwords that have a right boundary index equal to the index of the end of the word. With proper memoization, it is evident that for a word of size $|v|$, there are $|v|$ subproblems to solve. In addition, because each interval's right boundary corresponds to the word size, each interval is iterated over a constant number of times. As such, for word v, the total, memoized complexity of this segmentation is $\mathcal{O}(v + |A_v|)$ where A_v indicates the pre-segmentation subwords that are substrings of word v.

Algorithm 1 presents the subword segmentation algorithm. The algorithm takes as input a word and a collection of intervals corresponding to index boundaries of candidate subwords within the word. It then proceeds to select a set of intervals that maximally cover the word while utilizing the fewest number of intervals. Solutions to subproblems are memoized as to avoid repeated computation.

3.3 Hierarchical Subword Segmentation

In Subsection 3.1 we introduced the concept of utilizing high-entropy boundaries to create a subword vocabulary, and in Subsection 3.2 we introduce an algorithm for segmenting words into subwords based on the principle of parsimonious disjoint interval covering. In this subsection we demonstrate a high-level overview on how applying these two methods can be used to hierarchically segment words into multi-granular subwords.

Following the steps from Subsection 3.1, an initial subword vocabulary is created. Within the vocabulary, we differentiate between prefixes, suffixes, and root words. As seen in Algorithm 2, Line 2, each subword found in the input word is mapped to an interval indicating its boundary indices within the word with the condition that prefix intervals must start at the beginning of the word, suffix intervals must terminate at the end of the word, and root word intervals can be located at any position within the word. In addition, the complete word is not included (to ensure the word segments to smaller subwords). The algo-

---

Algorithm 1: DP Parsimonious Segmentation (DP)

Input: Word v, Subword Intervals A_v
Output: Optimal segmentation S

```
1  n[0] ← 0; c[0] ← 0; p[0] ← null;
2  for j := 1 to N_v do
3      num ← n[j-1]; cov←c[j-1]; pair ← p[j-1];
4      for (i, j) ∈ A_v do
5          cov' ← c[i-1]+(j-i+1)
6          num' ← n[i-1]+1
7          if cov' > cov then
8              cov ← cov'; num ← num';
9              pair ← (i, j);
10         end
11         if cov'=cov ∧ num'<num then
12             num ← num'; pair ← (i, j)
13         end
14     end
15     n[j] ← num; c[j] ← cov; p[j] ← pair;
16 end
17 return p
```

Algorithm 2: Segmentation Algorithm (SEGMENT)

Input: Word v, Subword Vocabulary SW
Output: Set of subwords of v

---

1   output $\leftarrow \{v\}$
2   $A_v \leftarrow \{(i, j) \text{ for } v_i \ldots v_j \in SW \text{ and j-i} \neq |v|\}$
3   **if** $A_v = \varnothing$ **then**
4 | **return** output
5   **end**
6   segmented $\leftarrow$ DP(w, A_v)
7   **for** subword $\in$ segmented **do**
8 | output $\cup$ SEGMENT(subword, SW)
9   **end**
10   **return** output

---

rithm terminates if the word cannot be further segmented. Otherwise, the word is segmented with the dynamic programming parsimonious segmentation algorithm. Each subword is then treated as a word and recursively segmented by the algorithm, and the collection of all subwords from segmentation are outputted.

3.4 Word Embedding

To efficiently utilize our mined subwords to improve upon word embeddings, we modify the Fast-Text model for word embeddings to use our extracted subwords (Bojanowski et al., 2016).

FastText utilizes the skip-gram objective with negative sampling yielding the following objective (for simplicity, $\ell(x) = \log(1 + \exp(-x))$):

$$\sum_{x=1}^{W} \left[\sum_{c \in \mathcal{C}_x} \ell(s(w_x, w_c)) + \sum_{t \in \mathcal{N}_{x,c}} \ell(-s(w_x, t)) \right] \tag{4}$$

The scoring function is then adapted to incorporate subword information as follows:

$$s(w_x, w_c) = \sum_{p \in w_x} \mathbf{z}_p^\mathsf{T} \mathbf{v}_c \tag{5}$$

which equates to a simple summation over subword embedding vectors.

4 Related Works

There have been many attempts at automatic substructure extraction from words. These techniques generally fall into one of three families: scoring based on segment predictability, identifying subwords based on discovering similar and dissimilar word parts, and optimization methods.

In morphological analysis of relating phonemes to morphemes, segment predictability has been suggested as a potential identifying characteristic for detecting subword structure. An early quantitative metric proposed was the number of different variations of subwords following a subword sequence whereby a high number of variations indicates a subword boundary (Harris, 1970). While this work provided influential insight into useful metrics for subword-detection, the main objective was developing a scoring function for identifying candidate subwords, not segmentation. Following this line of work, many methods have extended the variation boundary approach to identify frequent morphemes from text corpora (Hafer and Weiss, 1974). A similar method adopts the metric to identify frequent affixes (Déjean, 1998). Both these methods seek to identify a small subset of high-quality, high frequency subwords from each corpus, prioritizing precision over recall. Other methods propose slight variations to the predictability metric such as drops in transitional probabilities (Saffran et al., 1996).

Deviating from predictability-based methods, several subword detection methods have been proposed for detecting subwords by comparing words and identifying similar and dissimilar parts. One such method performs alignment from the left and right edge of words (Neuvel and Fulop, 2002) identifying common subwords. Another method adds words to a trie in correct order and reverse order to identify leading and trailing frequent subwords (Schone and Jurafsky, 2001). Unfortunately both these methods can only identify prefix and suffix subwords, ignoring many internal subwords. Unlike these methods, our subword segmentation is position insensitive and can identify subwords that occur in any position in a word.

Opting for an optimization over a scoring perspective, a variety of methods have been proposed. One such method models segmentation through the minimum description length principle (Creutz and Lagus, 2002). This method attempts to minimize both the vocabulary while maintaining the likelihood of the corpus data.This method was successfully applied to languages such as Turkish (Sak et al., 2010). Unfortunately, unlike methods that take the vocabulary as input, these family of optimization methods must make several passes over the corpus. This not only adds significant runtime and may discourage use as a preprocessing step before embedding, but can also be intractable for large text corpora. Other methods apply a maximum likelihood approach to identifying subwords (also called wordpieces) and has been successfully applied to a variety of NLP tasks (Wu et al., 2016; Schuster and Nakajima, 2012). And similarly the byte-pair compression algorithm has been used to identify subwords for neural machine translation tasks (Sennrich et al., 2015). Both these methods construct a fixed-size subword vocabulary to construct each word as a sequence of subwords.

Many attempts have been proposed to address data-sparsity when learning distributed word representations. These methods posit that individual words have semantically meaningful attributes that are shared among other words allowing for parameter sharing between vocabulary words. One such method proposes a factored neural language model where words are represented as a set of features including subword information (Alexandrescu and Kirchhoff, 2006). Another method attempts to incorporate morphological information into the word embeddings by adding morphological similarity features into a neural network along with the context features (Cui et al., 2015). This method while similarly motivated, does not leverage subword structure but instead utilizes the embeddings of "morphologically similar" words in the embedding process. While this may seem appealing, identifying morphologically similar words can be an expensive process as it requires a search over the entire vocabulary which may be prohibitive during on-the-fly computation out-of-word vocabulary. In addition, this method may miss important morphological cues such as negation subwords. When extended to use subword information, this model assumes subwords are already provided, this requires manual identification of subwords which can be an expensive human-powered task, especially in domain-specific settings or new languages (Qiu et al., 2014). Along similar motivation, a method has been proposed where given an input of morphologically annotated data, log-bilinear models are trained to jointly predict context words and its morphological tag (Cotterell and Schütze, 2015). Despite displaying superior embedding performance on German corpora, this method once again requires human-labeling for tagging words. This limits applicability to domain-specific corpora and new languages where labeled data is scarce or expensive to obtain. The method that is is closest to our approach is the extension of FastText enriched with subword information (Bojanowski et al., 2017). This method extends the standard skip-gram model but utilizes character-ngram subword embeddings for parameter sharing. The major differences between SubwordMine and this method is that FastText embedding utilizes all character n-grams of user-specified lengths for subword embedding and performs a simple sum over their representations while SubwordMine performs unsupervised segmentation and applies a novel attention mechanism to combine the subword representations into word representations. Finally, utilizing subword information was shown to improve performance in machine translation (Sennrich et al., 2016).

Another spectrum of approaches address word sparsity through the use of characters as the base unit for embedding. Some approaches treat each word as a sequence of characters. and apply recurrent neural networks to the task of language modeling (Bojanowski et al., 2015; Sutskever et al., 2011). Other related models apply convolutional neural networks directly on characters (Kim et al., 2016).

5 Experimental Results

We introduce the datasets used and methods for comparison. We then describe our evaluations for both subword extraction and for word embedding performance.

5.1 Datasets and methods for comparison

Datasets

We use the following three datasets for evaluation purpose:

- **DBLP Abstracts**. Computer science abstracts containing 529K abstracts, 186K unique words, and 39M tokens.

- **DBLP Title**. Titles of computer science papers published in 20 conferences containing 44K titles, 5.5K unique words, and 351K tokens.

- **PubMed Abstracts**. Abstracts of research papers obtained from from PubMed Central containing 421K abstracts, 334K unique words and 5.8M tokens.

For baseline comparison methods to our proposed SubwordMine algorithm we utilize a unigram language model segmentation of 'wordpieces' and byte-pair encoding segmentation as

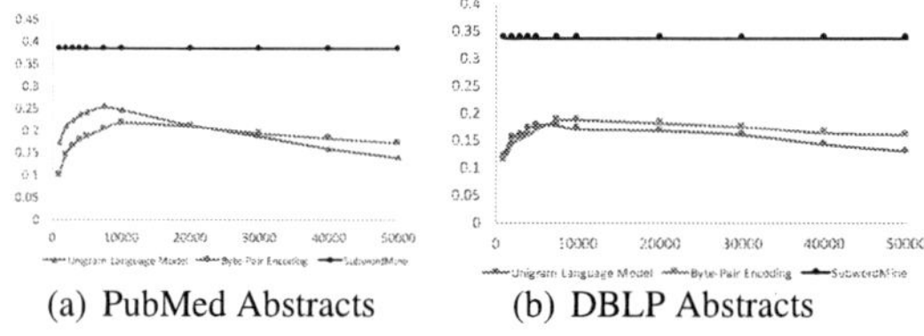

<table>
<tr><td align="center">(a) PubMed Abstracts</td><td align="center">(b) DBLP Abstracts</td></tr>
</table>

Figure 4: Accuracy in extracting Greek and Latin root words while varying subword vocabulary size.

Model	Extraction Accuracy	
	PubMed	DBLP
Byte-Pair Encoding	0.2180	0.1881
Unigram LM	0.2535	0.1782
SubwordMine	**0.3831**	**0.3363**

Table 1: Accuracy in automatically extracting Greek and Latin root words.

described in the related works. For comparable methods for embedding we utilize FastText, a proposed variation of the Skip-Gram objective that utilize subword information, and modify FastText to use a variety of subword segmentations.

5.2 Subword Extraction Accuracy

To evaluate the effectiveness of our proposed unsupervised segmentation algorithm at extracting semantically meaningful subwords, we collect a list of approximately three-thousand English words and their Greek or Latin roots. For each segmentor trained on each dataset, we test to see if the segmentation correctly extracts the ground truth root.

As seen in Figure 4, the accuracy of extracting the root words varies with the vocabulary size for both BPE and the Unigram LM method. As seen in Table 2, for the optimal vocabulary size for both methods, we see SubwordMine still outperforms both methods.

5.3 Perplexity

We investigate the benefits of using semantically meaningful subwords for parameter-sharing during when learning word embeddings. For each set subword-enriched embedding vectors, we learn a language model and evaluate its quality by computing the language model perplexity on a DBLP title dataset. The model used for language modeling is an LSTM variant of a recurrent neural network with two hidden layers and 600 hidden units per layer and regularized with dropout with

Model	Perplexity	
	Untuned	Tuned
SkipGram	378.45	245.01
BPE-FastText	356.29	210.59
ULM-FastText	324.07	220.73
FastText	370.68	212.88
SubwordMine	**320.65**	**207.84**

Table 2: Test perplexity on the language modeling task for DBLP titles dataset. Evaluation is performed with fixed pre-trained embeddings, and embedding tuning.

0.2 probability. The RNNs are unrolled for 35 steps and the batch size is set to 20. Parameters are learned using Adagrad with a gradient clipping of 1. Each language model instance trained on a training set partition consisting of 80% of the DBLP data and evaluation of perplexity was computed for each model on an independent test set consisting of 10% of the data after selecting the best performing iteration of the model on the remaining validation set.

The results are summarized in Table 2. Because our implementation performs minimal data cleaning and does not drop infrequent or out-of-vocabulary words, we expect the resulting perplexity should be relatively higher than cleaned-datasets but directly comparable among the differing methods (Bojanowski et al., 2016).

For the LSTM model, we observe that across all sub-word enriched embeddings perform better in language modeling over traditional skip-gram. Additionally, for both the untuned and tuned settings, SubwordMine segmentations improve test-perplexity over all other subword extraction method including original FastText's enumeration of all possible subwords. This is likely due to the sheer number of enumerated subwords and subword embeddings generated by FastText which may be more difficult to learn.

6 Conclusions

In this paper, we propose a computationally efficient method of segmenting vocabulary lists into semantically meaningful subwords. We demonstrate experimentally that utilizing the subwords in word embeddings in scientific domain corpora improves embedding quality as measured by a downstream language modeling task.

7   Future Works

Currently SubwordMine applies unsupervised segmentation. While this has be shown to yield high-quality segmentations, one natural extension is to incorporate human-labeling and perform supervised segmentation. Another area of work is to utilize subword structures in a variety of sequential modeling tasks which could improve tasks such as entity typing, relation extraction, and machine translation where substructures can provide valuable signals.

References

Andrei Alexandrescu and Katrin Kirchhoff. 2006. Factored neural language models. In *Proceedings of the Human Language Technology Conference of the NAACL, Companion Volume: Short Papers*, pages 1–4. Association for Computational Linguistics.

Piotr Bojanowski, Edouard Grave, Armand Joulin, and Tomas Mikolov. 2016. Enriching word vectors with subword information. *arXiv preprint arXiv:1607.04606*.

Piotr Bojanowski, Edouard Grave, Armand Joulin, and Tomas Mikolov. 2017. Enriching word vectors with subword information. *Transactions of the Association for Computational Linguistics*, 5:135–146.

Piotr Bojanowski, Armand Joulin, and Tomas Mikolov. 2015. Alternative structures for character-level rnns. *Prof. ICLR*.

Ronan Collobert and Jason Weston. 2008. A unified architecture for natural language processing: Deep neural networks with multitask learning. In *Proceedings of the 25th international conference on Machine learning*, pages 160–167. ACM.

Ryan Cotterell and Hinrich Schütze. 2015. Morphological word-embeddings. In *HLT-NAACL*, pages 1287–1292.

Mathias Creutz and Krista Lagus. 2002. Unsupervised discovery of morphemes. In *Proceedings of the ACL-02 workshop on Morphological and phonological learning-Volume 6*, pages 21–30. Association for Computational Linguistics.

Qing Cui, Bin Gao, Jiang Bian, Siyu Qiu, Hanjun Dai, and Tie-Yan Liu. 2015. Knet: A general framework for learning word embedding using morphological knowledge. *ACM Transactions on Information Systems (TOIS)*, 34(1):4.

Hervé Déjean. 1998. Morphemes as necessary concept for structures discovery from untagged corpora. In *Proceedings of the Joint Conferences on New Methods in Language Processing and Computational Natural Language Learning*, pages 295–298. Association for Computational Linguistics.

Jeffrey L Elman. 1990. Finding structure in time. *Cognitive science*, 14(2):179–211.

Margaret A Hafer and Stephen F Weiss. 1974. Word segmentation by letter successor varieties. *Information storage and retrieval*, 10(11-12):371–385.

Zellig S Harris. 1970. From phoneme to morpheme. In *Papers in Structural and Transformational Linguistics*, pages 32–67. Springer.

Zhiheng Huang, Wei Xu, and Kai Yu. 2015. Bidirectional lstm-crf models for sequence tagging. *arXiv preprint arXiv:1508.01991*.

Armand Joulin, Edouard Grave, and Piotr Bojanowski Tomas Mikolov. 2017. Bag of tricks for efficient text classification. *EACL 2017*, page 427.

Yoon Kim, Yacine Jernite, David Sontag, and Alexander M Rush. 2016. Character-aware neural language models. In *AAAI*, pages 2741–2749.

Tomas Mikolov, Kai Chen, Greg Corrado, and Jeffrey Dean. 2013a. Efficient estimation of word representations in vector space. *arXiv preprint arXiv:1301.3781*.

Tomas Mikolov, Ilya Sutskever, Kai Chen, Greg S Corrado, and Jeff Dean. 2013b. Distributed representations of words and phrases and their compositionality. In *Advances in neural information processing systems*, pages 3111–3119.

Tomas Mikolov, Wen-tau Yih, and Geoffrey Zweig. 2013c. Linguistic regularities in continuous space word representations. In *hlt-Naacl*, volume 13, pages 746–751.

Sylvain Neuvel and Sean A Fulop. 2002. Unsupervised learning of morphology without morphemes. In *Proceedings of the ACL-02 workshop on Morphological and phonological learning-Volume 6*, pages 31–40. Association for Computational Linguistics.

Siyu Qiu, Qing Cui, Jiang Bian, Bin Gao, and Tie-Yan Liu. 2014. Co-learning of word representations and morpheme representations. In *COLING*, pages 141–150.

David E Rumelhart, Geoffrey E Hinton, Ronald J Williams, et al. 1988. Learning representations by back-propagating errors. *Cognitive modeling*, 5(3):1.

Jenny R Saffran, Elissa L Newport, and Richard N Aslin. 1996. Word segmentation: The role of distributional cues. *Journal of memory and language*, 35(4):606–621.

Haşim Sak, Murat Saraclar, and Tunga Güngör. 2010. Morphology-based and sub-word language modeling for turkish speech recognition. In *Acoustics Speech and Signal Processing (ICASSP), 2010 IEEE International Conference on*, pages 5402–5405. IEEE.

Patrick Schone and Daniel Jurafsky. 2001. Knowledge-free induction of inflectional morphologies. In *Proceedings of the second meeting of the North American Chapter of the Association for Computational Linguistics on Language technologies*, pages 1–9. Association for Computational Linguistics.

Mike Schuster and Kaisuke Nakajima. 2012. Japanese and korean voice search. In *Acoustics, Speech and Signal Processing (ICASSP), 2012 IEEE International Conference on*, pages 5149–5152. IEEE.

Rico Sennrich, Barry Haddow, and Alexandra Birch. 2015. Neural machine translation of rare words with subword units. *arXiv preprint arXiv:1508.07909*.

Rico Sennrich, Barry Haddow, and Alexandra Birch. 2016. Neural machine translation of rare words with subword units. *Proc. ACL*.

Claude E Shannon. 2001. A mathematical theory of communication. *ACM SIGMOBILE Mobile Computing and Communications Review*, 5(1):3–55.

Ilya Sutskever, James Martens, and Geoffrey E Hinton. 2011. Generating text with recurrent neural networks. In *Proceedings of the 28th International Conference on Machine Learning (ICML-11)*, pages 1017–1024.

Duyu Tang, Furu Wei, Nan Yang, Ming Zhou, Ting Liu, and Bing Qin. 2014. Learning sentiment-specific word embedding for twitter sentiment classification. In *ACL (1)*, pages 1555–1565.

Yonghui Wu, Mike Schuster, Zhifeng Chen, Quoc V Le, Mohammad Norouzi, Wolfgang Macherey, Maxim Krikun, Yuan Cao, Qin Gao, Klaus Macherey, et al. 2016. Google's neural machine translation system: Bridging the gap between human and machine translation. *arXiv preprint arXiv:1609.08144*.

Will Y Zou, Richard Socher, Daniel Cer, and Christopher D Manning. 2013. Bilingual word embeddings for phrase-based machine translation. In *Proceedings of the 2013 Conference on Empirical Methods in Natural Language Processing*, pages 1393–1398.

A Comparison of Character Neural Language Model and Bootstrapping for Language Identification in Multilingual Noisy Texts

Wafia Adouane[1], Simon Dobnik[1], Jean-Philippe Bernardy[1], and Nasredine Semmar[2]
[1]Department of Philosophy, Linguistics and Theory of Science (FLoV),
Centre for Linguistic Theory and Studies in Probability (CLASP), University of Gothenburg
[2]CEA, LIST, Vision and Content Engineering Laboratory Gif-sur-Yvette, France
`{wafia.adouane,simon.dobnik,jean-philippe.bernardy}@gu.se`
`nasredine.semmar@cea.fr`

Abstract

This paper seeks to examine the effect of including background knowledge in the form of character pre-trained neural language model (LM), and data bootstrapping to overcome the problem of unbalanced limited resources. As a test, we explore the task of language identification in mixed-language short non-edited texts with an under-resourced language, namely the case of Algerian Arabic for which both labelled and unlabelled data are limited. We compare the performance of two traditional machine learning methods and a deep neural networks (DNNs) model. The results show that overall DNNs perform better on labelled data for the majority categories and struggle with the minority ones. While the effect of the untokenised and unlabelled data encoded as LM differs for each category, bootstrapping, however, improves the performance of all systems and all categories. These methods are language independent and could be generalised to other under-resourced languages for which a small labelled data and a larger unlabelled data are available.

1 Introduction

Most Natural Language Processing (NLP) tools are generally designed to deal with monolingual texts with more or less standardised spelling. However, users in social media, especially in multilingual societies, generate multilingual non-edited material where at least two languages or language varieties are used. This phenomenon is linguistically referred to as language (code) mixing where code-switching and borrowing, among others, are the most studied phenomena. Poplack and Meechan (1998) defined borrowing as a morphological or a phonological adaptation of a word from one language to another and code-switching as the use of a foreign word, as it is in its original language, to express something in another language. However, the literature does not make it clear whether the use of different script is counted as borrowing, or code-switching or something else. For instance, there is no linguistic well-motivated theory about how to classify languages written in other scripts, like French written in Arabic script which is frequently the case in North Africa. This theoretical gap could be explained by the fact that this fairly recent phenomenon has emerged with the widespread of the new technologies. In this paper, we consider both code-switching and borrowing and refer to them collectively as language mixing. Our motivation in doing so is to offer to sociolinguists a linguistically informative tool to analyse and study the language contact behaviour in the included languages.

The task of identifying languages in mixed-language texts is a useful pre-processing tool where sequences belonging to different languages/varieties are identified. They are then processed by further language/variety-specific tools and models. This task itself has neither been well studied for situations when many languages are mixed nor has it been explored as a main or an auxiliary task in multi-task learning (see Section 2).

1.1 Related Work

There has been some interesting work in detecting code mixing for a couple of languages/language varieties, mostly using traditional sequence labelling algorithms like Conditional Random Field (CRF), Hidden Markov Model (HMM), linear kernel Support Vector Machines (SVMs) and a combination of different methods and linguistic resources (Elfardy and Diab, 2012; Elfardy et al., 2013; Barman et al., 2014b,a; Diab et al., 2016; Samih and Maier, 2016; Adouane and Dobnik, 2017). Prior work that is most closely related to our work using neural networks and related languages, Samih et al. (2016) used supervised

Proceedings of the Second Workshop on Subword/Character LEvel Models, pages 22–31
New Orleans, Louisiana, June 6, 2018. ©2018 Association for Computational Linguistics

deep neural networks (LSTM) and a CRF classifier on the top of it to detect code-switching, using small datasets of tweets, between Egyptian Arabic and MSA and between Spanish and English using pre-trained word embeddings trained on larger datasets. However, in their annotation they combined ambiguous words, which are words that could be of either languages depending on the context, in one category called 'ambiguous' and ignored words from minority languages. Moreover, the system was evaluated on a dataset with no instances of neither 'ambiguous' nor 'mixed-language' words, basically distinguishing between MSA and Egyptian Arabic words in addition to Named Entities and other non-linguistic tokens like punctuation, etc.

Similar to our work, Kocmi and Bojar (2017) proposed a supervised bidirectional LSTM model. However, the data used to train the model was created by mixing edited texts, at a line level, in 131 languages written in different scripts to create a multilingual data, making it a very different task from the one investigated here. We use non-edited texts, a realistic data as generated by users reflecting the real use of the included languages which are all written in the same Arabic script. Our texts are shorter and the size of the dataset is smaller, therefore, our task is more challenging.

By comparison to our work, most of the literature focuses on detecting code-switching points in a text, either at a token level or at a phrase level or even beyond a sentence boundaries, we distinguish between borrowing and code-switching at a word level by assigning all borrowed words to a separate variety (BOR). Most importantly, our main focus is to investigate ways to inject extra knowledge to take advantage of the unlabelled data.

1.2 Linguistic Situation in Algeria

The linguistic landscape in Algeria consists of several languages which are used in different social and geographic contexts to different degrees (Adouane et al., 2016a): local Arabic varieties (ALG), Modern Standard Arabic (MSA) which is the only standardised Arabic variety, Berber which is an Afro-Asiatic language different from Arabic and widely spoken in North Africa, and other non-Arabic languages such as French, English, Spanish, Turkish, etc. A typical text consists of a mixture of these languages, and this mix-

ture is often referred to, somewhat mistakenly as Algerian Arabic. In this paper, we use the term Algerian language to refer to a mixture of languages and language varieties spoken in Algeria, and the term Algerian variety (ALG) to refer to the local variety of Arabic, which is used alongside other languages such as, for example Berber (BER).

This work seeks to identify the language or language variety of each word within an Algerian language text. Algerian language is characterised by non-standardised spelling and spelling variations based on the phonetic transcription of many local variants. For instance, the Algerian sentence in (1), which is user generated, is a mixture of 3 languages (Arabic, French and Berber) and 2 Arabic varieties (MSA and ALG). Each word is coloured by its language in d., b. is an IPA transcription and c. is the human English translation. To illustrate the difficulty of the problem, we additionally show the (incorrect) translation proposed by Google translate e., where words in black are additional words not appearing in the original sentence.

(1)   a. سيلتوبلي حل الطاقة و سكر لباب موراك

      b. [muræk ælbæb sekkær wu ætʕaqæ ħæl siːltupliː]

      c. Please open the window and close the door behind you

      d. French Algerian Berber MSA Berber MSA Algerian

      e. SELTOPLEY POWER SOLUTION AND SUGAR FOR MORAK PAPER

All the words in different languages are normally written in the Arabic script, which causes high degree of lexical ambiguity and therefore even if we had dictionaries (only available for MSA) it would be hard to disambiguate word senses this way. In (1), the ALG word حل *open* means *solution* in MSA, the Berber word الطاقة *window* which is adapted to the MSA morphology by adding the MSA definite article ال (case of borrowing) means *energy/capacity* in MSA. The Berber word سكر

close means *sugar / sweeten / liquor / get drunk* in MSA.

Moreover, the rich morphology of Arabic is challenging because it is a fusional language where suffixes and other morphemes are added to the base word, and a single morpheme denotes multiple aspects and features. Algerian Arabic shares many linguistic features with MSA, but it differs from it mainly phonologically, morphologically and lexically. For instance, a verb in the first person singular in ALG is the same as the first person plural in MSA. The absence of a morphological/syntactic analyser for ALG makes it challenging to correctly analyse an ALG text mixed with other languages and varieties.

Except for MSA, Arabic varieties are neither well-documented nor well-studied, and they are classified as under-resourced languages. Furthermore, social media are the only source of written texts for Algerian Arabic. The work in NLP on Algerian Arabic and other Arabic varieties also suffers severely from the lack of labelled (and even unlabelled) data that would allow any kind of supervised training. Another challenge is that we have to deal with all the complications present in social media domain, namely the use of short texts, spelling and word segmentation errors, etc. in addition to the non-standard orthography used in informal Arabic varieties. We see the task of identification of the variety of each word in a text a necessary first step towards developing more sophisticated NLP tools for this Arabic variety which is itself a mixture of other languages and varieties.

In this paper we explore two avenues for improving the state of the art in variety identification for Algerian Arabic. First, we measure the ability of recurrent neural networks to identify language mixing using only a limited training corpus. Second, we explore to what extent adding background knowledge in the form of pre-trained character-based language model and bootstrapping can be effective in dealing with under-resourced languages in the domain of language identification in mixed-language texts for which neither large labelled nor unlabelled datasets exist.

The paper is organized as follows: in Section 2, we give a brief overview of methods for levering learning from limited datasets. In Section 3, we describe the data. In Section 4, we present the architecture of our learning configurations which include both traditional approaches and deep neural networks and explain the training methods used on the labelled data, experiments and results. In Section 5, we experiment with these models when adding background knowledge and report the results.

2 Leveraging Limited Datasets

Deep learning has become the leading approach to solving linguistic tasks. However deep neural networks (DNNs) used in a supervised and unsupervised learning scenario usually require large datasets in order for the trained models to perform well. For example, Zhang et al. (2015) estimates that the size of the training dataset for character-level DNNs for text classification task should range from hundreds of thousands to several million of examples.

The limits imposed by the lack of labelled datasets have been countered by combining *structural learning* and *semi-supervised learning* (Ando and Zhang, 2005). Contrary to the supervised approach where a labelled dataset is used to train a model, in *structural learning*, the learner first learns underlying structures from either labelled or unlabelled data. If the model is trained on labelled data, it should be possible to reuse the knowledge encoded in the relations of the predictive features in this auxiliary task, if properly trained, to solve other related tasks. If the model is trained on unlabelled data, the model captures the underlying structures of words or characters in a language as a language model (LM), i.e., model the probabilistic distribution of words and characters of a text.

Such pre-trained LM should be useful for various supervised tasks assuming that linguistic structures are predictive of the labels used in these tasks. Approaches like this are known as *transfer learning* or *multi-task learning* (MTL) and are classified as a semi-supervised approaches (with no bootstrapping) (Zhou et al., 2004). There is an increasing interest in evaluating different frameworks (Ando and Zhang, 2005; Pan and Yang, 2010) and comparing neural network models (Cho et al., 2014; Yosinski et al., 2014). Some studies have shown that MTL is useful for certain tasks (Sutton et al., 2007) while others reported that it is not always effective (Alonso and Plank, 2017).

Bootstrapping (Nigam et al., 2000) is a general and commonly used method of countering the limits of labelled datasets for learning. It is a semi-supervised method where a well-performing model is used to automatically label new data which is subsequently used as a training data for another model. This helps to enhance supervised learning. However, this is also not always effective. For example, Pierce and Cardie (2001) and Ando and Zhang (2005) show that bootstrapping degraded the performance of some classifiers.

3 Data

In this section, we describe the datasets that we use for training and testing our models. We use two datasets: small dataset, annotated with language labels, and a larger dataset lacking such annotation.

3.1 Labelled data

We use the human labelled corpus described by Adouane and Dobnik (2017) where each word is tagged with one of the following labels: ALG (Algerian), BER (Berber), BOR (Borrowing), ENG (English), FRC (French), MSA (Modern Standard Arabic), NER (Named Entity), SND (interjections/sounds) and DIG (digits). The annotators have access to the full context for each word. To the best of our knowledge, this corpus is the only available labelled dataset for code-switching and borrowing in Algerian Arabic, written in Arabic script, and in fact also one of the very few available datasets for this particular language variety overall. Because of the limited annotation resources the corpus is small, containing only 10,590 samples (each sample is a short text, for example one post in a social media platform). In total, the data contains 215,875 tokens distributed unbalancely as follows: 55.10% ALG (representing the majority category with 118,960 words), 38.04% MSA (82,121 words), 2.80% FRC (6,049 words), 1.87% BOR (4,044 words), 1.05% NER (2,283 words), 0.64% DIG (1,392 numbers), 0.32% SND (691 tokens), 0.10% ENG (236 words), and 0.04% BER (99 words).

3.2 Unlabelled data

Unfortunately, there is no existing user-generated unlabelled textual corpus for ALG. Therefore, we also collected, automatically and manually, new content from social media in Algerian Arabic which include social networking sites, blogs, microblogs, forums, community media sites and user reviews.[1]

The new raw corpus contains mainly short non-edited texts which require further processing before useful information can be extracted from them. We cleaned and pre-processed the corpus following the pre-processing and normalisation methods described by Adouane and Dobnik (2017). The data pre-processing and normalisation is based on applying certain linguistic rules, including: 1. Removal of non-linguistic words like punctuation and emoticons (indeed emoticons and inconsistent punctuation are abundant in social media texts.) 2. Reducing all adjacent repeated letters to maximum two occurrences of letters, based on the principle that MSA allows no more than two adjacent occurrences of the same letter. 3. Removal of diacritics representing short vowels, because these are rarely used; 4. Removal all duplicated instances of texts; 5. Removal of texts not mainly written in Arabic script 6. Normalisation all remaining characters to the Arabic script. Indeed, some users use related scripts like Persian, Pashto or Urdu characters, either because of their keyboard layout or to express some sounds which do not exist in the Arabic alphabet, e.g. /p/, /v/ and /g/.

Additionally, we feed each document, as a whole, to a language identification system that distinguishes between the most popular Arabic varieties (Adouane et al., 2016b) including MSA; Moroccan (MOR); Tunisian (TUN); Egyptian (EGY); Levantine (LEV); Iraqi (IRQ) and Gulf (GUF) Arabic. We retain only those predicted to be Algerian language, so that we can focus on language identification within Algerian Arabic, at the word level.

Table 1 gives some statistics about the labelled and unlabelled datasets. Texts refer to short texts from social media, words to linguistic words excluding punctuation and other tokens, and types to sets of words or unique words. We notice that 82.52% of the words occur less than 10 times in both datasets. This is due to the high variation of spelling and misspellings which are common in these kinds of texts.

Dataset	#Texts	#Words	#Types
Labelled	10,590	213,792	57,054
Unlabelled	189,479	3,270,996	290,629

Table 1: Information about datasets.

4 Using Labelled Data

4.1 Systems and Models

We frame the task as a sequence labelling problem, namely to assign each word in a sequence the label of the language that the word has in that context. We use three different approaches: two existing sequence labelling systems – (i) an HHM-based sequence labeller (Adouane and Dobnik, 2017); (ii) a classification-based system with various back-off strategies from (Adouane and Dobnik, 2017) which previously performed best on this task, henceforth called the state-of-the-art system; and (iii) a new system using deep neural networks (DNNs).

4.1.1 HMM system

The HMM system is a classical probabilistic sequence labelling system based on Hidden Markov Model where the probability of a label is estimated based on the history of the observations, previous words and previous labels. In order to optimise the probabilities and find the best sequence of labels based on a sequence of words, the Viterbi algorithm is used. For words that have not been seen in the training data, an constant low probability computed from the training data is assigned.

4.1.2 State-of-the-art system

The best-so-far performing system for identifying language mixing in Algerian texts is described by Adouane and Dobnik (2017). The system is a classifier-based model that predicts the language or variety of each word in the input text with various back-off-strategies: trigram and bigram classification, lexicon lookup from fairly large manually compiled and curated lexicons, manually-defined rules capturing linguistic knowledge based on word affixes, word length and character combinations, and finally the most frequent class (unigram).

4.1.3 DNN model

Recurrent Neural Networks (RNNs) (Elman, 1990) have been used extensively in sequence prediction. The most popular RNN variants are the Long Short-Term Memory (LSTMs) (Hochreiter and Schmidhuber, 1997) and the Gated Recurrent Unit (GRUs) (Cho et al., 2014).

Our neural networks consists of four layers: one embedding layer, two recurrent layers, and a dense layer with softmax activation. All our models are optimized using the *Adam* optimizer, built using the *Keras* library (Chollet, 2015), and run using a TensorFlow backend. A summary of the model architecture is shown in Figure 1. (This variant is composed of only the uncoloured (white) parts of the figure; the coloured parts are added in the model described in section 5). The DNN is provided the input character by character. We opt for character-based input rather than word-based input for two reasons. First, we expect that the internal structure of words (phonemes and morphemes) is predictive of a particular variety. This way we hope to capture contexts within words and across words. Second, we do not have to worry about the size of the vocabulary, which we would if we were to use word embeddings.

This language-identification model is trained end-to-end. Because of the nature of RNNs, the network will assign one language variant per input symbol, and thus per character — even though the tags are logically associated word-by-word. To deal with this mismatch, when training we tag each character of a word and the space which follows it with the variant of the word. When evaluating the model, we use the tag associated with the space, so that all the word has been fed to the model before a prediction is made.

We have trained models with various values for the hyper-parameters: number of layers, number of epochs, memory size, drop-out rate and the batch size, but report detailed results for the model with the best behaviour. We experimented with both GRU and LSTM RNNs and found that the GRU performs better than LSTM on our task which is in line with the results of the previous comparisons but on different tasks (Chung et al., 2014). We also found out that our best systems are optimised with the architecture shown in Figure 1 with a memory size of 200, batch size of 512 and number of epochs of 25. Increasing or decreasing these values caused the overall accuracy to drop. Using drop-out improved the performance of the systems (overall accuracy $> 90\%$) over not using it ($< 70\%$). The best results are obtained using drop-out rate of 0.2 for the recurrent layers. We refer to this model as *DNN* in the following.

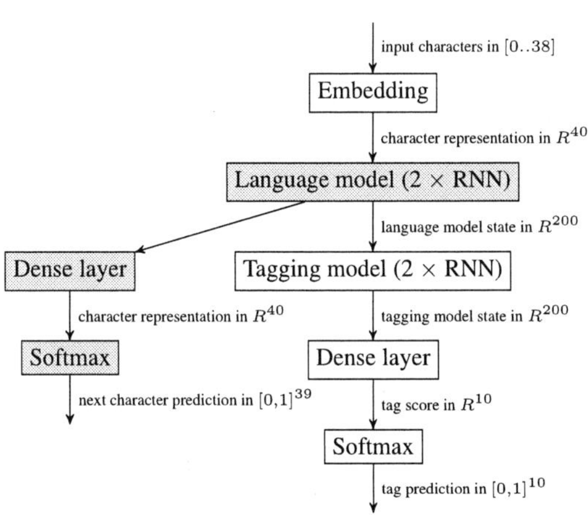

Figure 1: DNN architecture.

4.2 Results

To ensure a fair comparison, all the models have been evaluated under the same conditions. We use 10-fold cross validation on all of them and report their performance measured as the average accuracy. Table 2 shows the results. Note that for the DNN we only report the results of the (best-performing) GRU models. As a baseline we take the most frequent category in the labelled data. State-of-the-art (2) outperforms slightly HMM (1). DNN (3) outperforms slightly the State-of-the-art (2). All the systems perform better than the baseline.

	Model	Accuracy (%)
1	HMM	89.29
2	State-of-the-art	89.83
3	DNN	**90.53**
4	Baseline	55.10

Table 2: Performance of the models on labelled data.

Figure 2 shows the performance of each model per category reported as average F-score. Overall the models perform better on the majority categories such as ALG (Algerian) and MSA (Modern Standard Arabic), and non linguistic categories like DIG (digits) and SND (sounds) because their patterns are more or less regular and language independent. The State-of-the-art system achieves the best performances for all categories except for ALG where it is slightly outperformed by DNN,

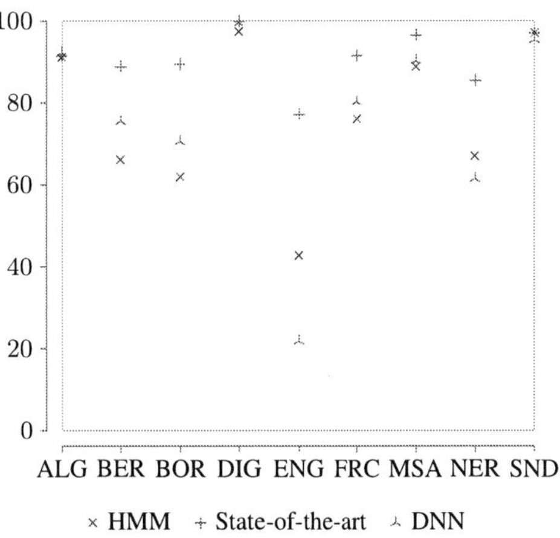

Figure 2: Models' average F-score per category.

average F-score of 91.45 and 92.22 respectively. A possible explanation for this is that the State-of-the-art system is more robust because it involves several strategies of classification. DNN performed better than HMM in all cases except for ENG (English) and SND. Both DNN and HMM struggle with minority categories like ENG, BOR (borrowing), BER (Berber), NER (Named Entities), and FRC (French). Note that in this experiment we only used the smaller labelled dataset. In the following section, we explore ways to take advantage of the additional relatively large unlabelled dataset in order to improve the performance of the systems.

5 Using Data Augmentation With Background Knowledge

5.1 Training Methods

In this section, we examine which data augmentation method performed on the unlabelled corpus can best enhance the performance of our three models. We experiment with data bootstrapping, pre-training a language model, and the combination of both methods. In each case, we are providing some form of background knowledge compared to the task described in Section 4.

5.1.1 Bootstrapping

For bootstrapping, we use the State-of-the-art system (Section 4.1.2) to label the unlabelled data without additional checking of the quality of annotation and then use this bootstrapped data in further training. We re-run the experiments described in Section 4 using the bootstrapped data as the training data. We refer to the systems as *HMM bootstrapped*, *State-of-the-art bootstrapped*, and *DNN bootstrapped* respectively.

5.1.2 Language Model

Another way to take advantage of the unlabelled data is to train a language model (LM) on the whole data and use the internal state of the LM as input to the tagger, rather than using the raw textual input. To this end, we modify the structure of our DNN as indicated by the blue-coloured parts in Figure 1. Namely, we add two language-modelling RNN layers between the embedding and the tagging layers. They are followed by a dense layer with softmax activation, which predicts the next character in the input.

With this setup, we train the language-modelling layers on the unlabelled corpus, as a generative language model on the unlabelled data set. Thus, the output of these layers contains the information necessary to predict the next character given the previous sequence of characters. The language model is trained on 80% of the unlabelled data and evaluated on the remaining 20%. The rest of the network is then trained as in the previous case (Section 4.1.3). We stress that, in this instance, only the last two layers are trained on the language-identification task. We refer to this model as *DNN with LM*.

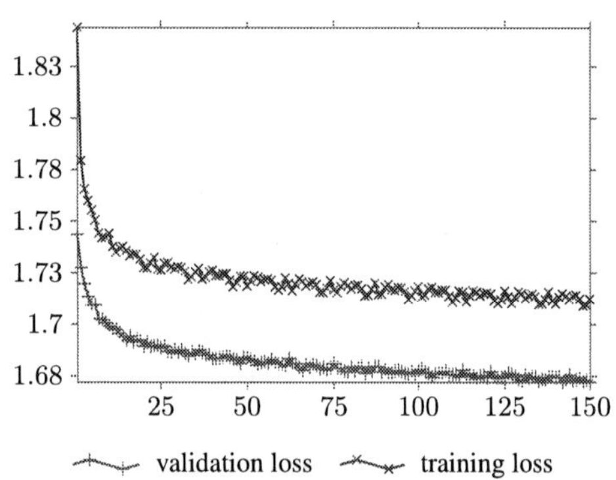

Figure 3: Language model loss through training epochs

You may notice in Figure 3 that the model is still improving (at 150 epochs), albeit slowly, even after exhausting our computational budget. Nevertheless, the model appears to be working well as a text generator. For instance, we took sentence (1) as a seed and obtained sentences that are grammatically and structurally acceptable, even if they are semantically meaningless and reproduce the

many spelling variants found in the original corpus. Here are two examples:

1. المهم انا ما نقدرش نموت عليها و الله يا ختي راني معاك و الله ما نقولك انا ما نقدرش نتعلم من الحال

2. و الله ما نقول الله يبارك ما يعرفش يتبلاو و يعرف وين راه المرا الي ما يحبش يحب يقول الله يهدينا

5.1.3 Language Model and Bootstrapping

We retrain the DNN model using the pre-trained LM and the bootstrapped data in order to optimise the use of the unlabelled data. We refer to this model as *DNN bootstrapped and LM*.

5.2 Results

We evaluate all the models under the same conditions as in Section 4, using 10-fold cross validation we report the average accuracy over the folds. The evaluation set in the bootstrapping models in each fold is only taken from the labelled data while the training part consists of a combined 9-folds from the labelled data and the entire bootstrapped data. In other words, the entire bootstrapped data is added to the training data at each time. In the case of DNNs, we found again that GRUs perform significantly better than LSTM, and that bootstrapped models are optimised with drop-out rate of 0.2 whereas models with language model perform better with drop-out rate of 0.1. The obtained results are reported as the average accuracy in Table 3. For the DNN, we only report the results of the (best-performing) GRU models.

	Model	Accuracy (%)
1	HMM bootstrapped	93.97
2	State-of-the-art bootstrapped	**95.42**
3	DNN bootstrapped	93.31
4	DNN with LM	90.31
5	DNN bootstrapped and LM	90.19

Table 3: Performance of the models with background knowledge.

The best performance overall is achieved by the bootstrapped state-of-of-the-art model (2). HMM bootstrapped (1) performs slightly better than the DNN bootstrapped (3). Bootstrapping helps the State-of-the-art system and HMM more than DNN. This is due to the training nature of the DNN which is based on capturing frequent regular patterns, hence adding the bootstrapped data means introducing even more irregular patterns.

Compared to the results in Section 4.2, the DNN bootstrapped (3) outperforms all the models with the labelled data: (1), (2) and (3) in Table 2. The bootstrapping method thus improves the performance of all configurations, whether they are using DNNs or not. The reported benefits of bootstrapping are contrary to the previous observations where bootstrapping did not help (Section 2).

However, the use of the language model (4) decreases slightly (-0.22%) the performance of the DNN compared to its performance with the labelled data (3) in Table 2. The use of the bootstrapping and the language model (5) leads to no significant difference in performance in respect to (4). Overall, it appears that the usage of the language model has no strong effect. This could be caused by the noise in the data, and adding more unlabelled data makes it hard for the language model to learn all the data irregularities. Maybe the system requires more training data.

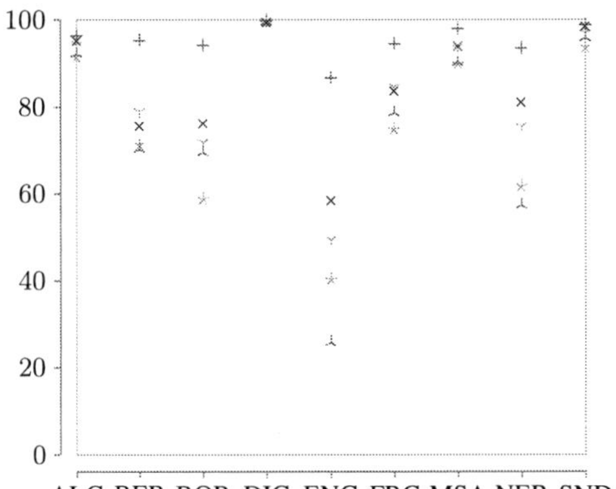

Figure 4: Models' average F-score per category.

Figure 4 sums up the performance of each model per category reported as the average F-score. The first thing to notice is that bootstrapping improves the performance of all systems, and the best performance is achieved with the State-of-the-art. This could be explained by 'the more data, the better performance'. HMM bootstrapped outperforms the DNN bootstrapped except for FRC and BER. Adding language model to the DNN causes the overall accuracy to drop compared to the DNN bootstrapped. Nevertheless, compared to the results in Figure 2, language model behaves differently with each category. For instance, it boosts the performance of the DNN on ENG, and the performance on BOR, BER, FRC over HMM. Whereas combining language model and bootstrapped data performs the worst except for BER, ENG and NER. The effect of combining bootstrapping and language model is better for minority categories: BER, ENG and NER.

Error analysis of the confusion matrices shows that all the systems are confused, chiefly between ALG and MSA, BOR and ALG, FRC and ALG. The confusions are caused mainly by the lexical ambiguity between these categories, given that we identify the language of each word in its context.

6 Conclusions

We have examined the automatic classification of language identification in mixed-language texts on limited datasets of Algerian Arabic, in particular a small unbalanced labelled dataset and a slightly larger unlabelled dataset. We tested whether the inclusion of a pre-trained LM on the unlabelled dataset and bootstrapping the unlabelled dataset can leverage the performance of the systems. Overall when using only the small labelled data, DNNs outperformed the HMM and the State-of-the-art system. However, DNNs performed better on the majority categories and struggled with the minority ones in comparison to the State-of-the-art system. Bootstrapping improved the performance of all models, both DNNs and not DNNs for all categories.

Adding a background knowledge in the form of a pre-trained LM to DNNs had a different effect per category. While it boosted the performance of the minority categories, its effect on the majority ones was not clear. Despite the generative behaviour of the LM, tested in Section 5.1.2, which showed that LM did learn the underlying structures of the unlabelled data, the effect of the encoded knowledge maybe was not suitable for our main task. This could be also caused by the high noise level in the data, even though deep learning is generally thought to handle noise well.

In our future work, we will focus on exploring (i) different DNN configurations to investigate the best ways of injecting background knowledge as well as (ii) different data pre-processing methods to normalise spelling and remove misspellings for MSA, and deal with word segmentation errors.

Acknowledgement

The research reported in this paper was supported by a grant from the Swedish Research Council (VR project 2014-39) for the establishment of the Centre for Linguistic Theory and Studies in Probability (CLASP) at the University of Gothenburg.

References

Wafia Adouane and Simon Dobnik. 2017. *Proceedings of the Third Arabic Natural Language Processing Workshop*, chapter Identification of Languages in Algerian Arabic Multilingual Documents. Association for Computational Linguistics.

Wafia Adouane, Nasredine Semmar, Richard Johansson, and Victoria Bobicev. 2016a. Automatic Detection of Arabicized Berber and Arabic Varieties. pages 63–72. The COLING 2016 Organizing Committee.

Wafia Adouane, Nasredine Semmar, Richard Johansson, and Victoria Bobicev. 2016b. Automatic Detection of Arabicized Berber and Arabic Varieties. In *Proceedings of the Third Workshop on NLP for Similar Languages, Varieties and Dialects*, pages 63–72.

Héctor Martìnez Alonso and Barbara Plank. 2017. When is Multitask Learning Effective? Semantic Sequence Prediction under Varying Data Conditions. In *EACL (long)*.

Rie Kubota Ando and Tong Zhang. 2005. A Framework for Learning Predictive Structures from Multiple Tasks and Unlabeled Data. *The Journal of Machine Learning Research*, 6:1817–1853.

Utsab Barman, Amitava Das, Joachim Wagner, and Jennifer Foster. 2014a. Code-mixing: A challenge for Language Identification in the Language of Social Media. In *In Proceedings of the First Workshop on Computational Approaches to Code-Switching*.

Utsab Barman, Joachim Wagner, Grzegorz Chrupala, and Jennifer Foster. 2014b. Dcu-uvt: Word-Level Language Classification with Code-Mixed Data.

Kyunghyun Cho, Bart Van Merrienboer, Caglar Gulcehre, Dzmitry Bahdanau, Fethi Bougares, Holger Schwenk, and Yoshua Bengio. 2014. *Learning Phrase Representations Using RNN Encoder-Decoder for Statistical Machine Translation*. arXiv preprint arXiv:1406.1078.

François Chollet. 2015. Keras. `https://github.com/fchollet/keras`.

Junyoung Chung, Caglar Gulcehre, KyungHyun Cho, and Yoshua Bengio. 2014. *Empirical Evaluation of Gated Recurrent Neural Networks on Sequence Modeling*. arXiv:1412.3555.

Mona Diab, Pascale Fung, Mahmoud Ghoneim, Julia Hirschberg, and Thamar Solorio. 2016. *Proceedings of the Second Workshop on Computational Approaches to Code Switching*. Association for Computational Linguistics, Austin, Texas.

Heba Elfardy, Mohamed Al-Badrashiny, and Mona Diab. 2013. Code Switch Point Detection in Arabic. In *Proceedings of the 18th International Conference on Application of Natural Language to Information Systems (NLDB2013)*.

Heba Elfardy and Mona Diab. 2012. Token Level Identification of Linguistic Code Switching. In *COLING*, pages 287–296.

Jeffrey L. Elman. 1990. Finding Structure in Time. *Cognitive Science*, 14(2):179–211.

Sepp Hochreiter and Juergen Schmidhuber. 1997. Long Short-Term Memory. *Neural Computation*, 9(8):1735–1780.

Tom Kocmi and Ondřej Bojar. 2017. Lanidenn: Multilingual Language Identification on Text Stream. In *Proceedings of the 15th Conference of the European Chapter of the Association for Computational Linguistics: Volume 1, Long Papers*, pages 927–936. Association for Computational Linguistics.

Kamal Nigam, Andrew Kachites McCallum, Sebastian Thrun, and Tom Mitchell. 2000. Text Classification from Labeled and Unlabeled Documents Using EM. *Machine Learning, Special issue on Information Retrieval*, pages 103–134.

Sinno Jialin Pan and Qiang Yang. 2010. A Survey on Transfer Learning. *IEEE Transactions on Knowledge and Data Engineering*, 22(10).

David Pierce and Claire Cardie. 2001. Limitations of Co-training for Natural Language Learning from Large Datasets. In *Proceedings of the 2001 Conference on Empirical Methods in Natural Language Processing (EMNLP)*.

Shana Poplack and Marjory Meechan. 1998. How Languages Fit Together in Codemixing. *The International Journal of Bilingualism*, 2(2):127–138.

Younes Samih, Suraj Maharjan, Mohammed Attia, Laura Kallmeyer, and Thamar Solorio. 2016. Multilingual code-switching identification via lstm recurrent neural networks. In *Proceedings of the Second Workshop on Computational Approaches to Code Switching*, pages 50–59.

Younes Samih and Wolfgang Maier. 2016. Detecting Code-Switching in Moroccan Arabic. In *Proceedings of SocialNLP @ IJCAI-2016*.

Charles Sutton, Andrew McCallum, and Khashayar Rohanimanesh. 2007. Dynamic Conditional Random Fields: Factorized Probabilistic Models for Labeling and Segmenting Sequence Data. *Journal of Machine Learning Research*, 8(Mar):693–723.

Jason Yosinski, Jeff Clune, Yoshua Bengio, and Hod Lipson. 2014. How Transferable are Features in Deep Neural Networks? *In Advances in Neural Information Processing Systems 27 (NIPS '14), NIPS Foundation.*

Xiang Zhang, Junbo Zhao, and Yann LeCun. 2015. *Character-level Convolutional Networks for Text Classification.* Advances in Neural Information Processing Systems 28 (NIPS 2015).

Dengyong Zhou, Olivier Bousquet, Thomas Navin Lal, Jason Weston, and Bernhard Schölkopf. 2004. *Learning with Local and Global Consistency.* In NIPS 2003.

Addressing Low-Resource Scenarios with Character-aware Embeddings

Sean Papay and **Sebastian Padó** and **Ngoc Thang Vu**
Institut für Maschinelle Sprachverarbeitung
Universität Stuttgart, Germany
{sean.papay,pado,thangvu}@ims.uni-stuttgart.de

Abstract

Most modern approaches to computing word embeddings assume the availability of text corpora with billions of words. In this paper, we explore a setup where only corpora with millions of words are available, and many words in any new text are out of vocabulary. This setup is both of practical interest – modeling the situation for specific domains and low-resource languages – and of psycholinguistic interest, since it corresponds much more closely to the actual experiences and challenges of human language learning and use. We evaluate skip-gram word embeddings and two types of character-based embeddings on word relatedness prediction. On large corpora, performance of both model types is equal for frequent words, but character awareness already helps for infrequent words. Consistently, on small corpora, the character-based models perform overall better than skip-grams. The concatenation of different embeddings performs best on small corpora and robustly on large corpora.

1 Introduction

State-of-the-art word embedding models are routinely trained on very large corpora. For example, Mikolov et al. (2013a) train word2vec on a corpus of 6 billion tokens, and Pennington et al. (2014) report the best GloVe results on 42 billion tokens.

From a language technology perspective, it is perfectly reasonable to use large corpora where available. However, even with large corpora, embeddings struggle to accurately model the meaning of infrequent words (Luong et al., 2013). Moreover, for the vast majority of languages, substantially less data is available. For example, there are only 4 languages with Wikipedias larger than 1 billion words,[1] and 25 languages with more than 100 million words. Similarly, specialized domains even in very high-resource languages are bound to have much less data available.

From a psycholinguistic point of view, current models miss the crucial ability of the human language faculty to generalize from little data. By seventh grade, students have only heard about 50 million spoken words, and read about 3.8 million tokens of text, acquiring a vocabulary of 40,000–100,000 words (Landauer and Dumais, 1997). This also means that any new text likely contains out-of-vocabulary words which students interpret by generalizing from existing knowledge – an ability that plain word embedding models lack.

There are some studies that have focused on modeling infrequent and unseen words by capturing information at the subword and character levels. Luong et al. (2013) break words into morphemes, and use recursive neural networks to compose word meanings from morpheme meanings. Similarly, Bojanowski et al. (2017) represent words as bags of character n-grams, allowing morphology to inform word embeddings without requiring morphological analysis. However, both models are still typically applied to large corpora of training data, with the smallest English corpora used comprising about 1 billion tokens.

Our study investigates how embedding models fare when applied to much smaller corpora, containing only millions of words. Few studies, except Sahlgren and Lenci (2016), have considered this setup in detail. We evaluate one word-based and two character-based embedding models on word relatedness tasks for English and German. We find that that the character-based models mimics human learning more closely, with both better results on small datasets and better performance on rare words. At the same time, a fused representation that takes both word and character level into account yields the best results for small corpora.

---

[1] https://en.wikipedia.org/wiki/List_of_Wikipedias#Detailed_list (as of 9 Jan 2018)

Proceedings of the Second Workshop on Subword/Character LEvel Models, pages 32–37
New Orleans, Louisiana, June 6, 2018. ©2018 Association for Computational Linguistics

WL	
Window size	5
Negative samples	15
Word embedding dim.	300
Minimum word count as inclusion as target	5 for full, 1 for small corpora
Starting learning rate	0.025
Training epochs	5 for full, 15 for 100 MiB, 75 for 10 MiB corpora

FT	
Word embedding dim.	300
Training epochs	5
Learning rate	0.05
Minimum n-gram length	3
Maximum n-gram length	6
Negative samples	5

CL	
Word length	16 characters
Character embedding dim.	15
Convolution filter widths	$\langle 1, 2, 3, 4, 5, 6, 7 \rangle$
Convolution filter units	$\langle 200, 200, 200, 200, 250, 300, 350 \rangle$
Word embedding dim.	300
Minimum word count for inclusion as context	5
Batch size	100
Learning rate	0.05
Training epochs	as above

CAT	
Word embedding dim.	$300 + 300 + 300 = 900$

Table 1: Hyperparameters (dim. = dimensionality). For WL and FT, software defaults were used for all hyperparameters unless otherwise specified.

2 Models

We examine four models for generating our word embeddings. All of the use a skip-gram objective function but differ in the granularity of linguistic input that they model: the first model works at the word level (WL); the second model, fastText (FT), works at the character n-gram level; the third model is character-based (CL); the forth model is a fusion of the first three (CAT). The hyperparameters of the models are shown in Table 1.

2.1 Word-level Skip-gram Model

As a character-agnostic model, we use a standard, word-level skip-gram model (WL, Mikolov et al. 2013a), with negative sampling loss. All in-vocabulary words are assigned an embedding; out-of-vocabulary words are assigned the vector average of all in-vocabulary embeddings. We use the word2vec software for our WL model[2].

2.2 fastText

The fastText (FT) model was introduced in Bojanowski et al. (2017). This model is based upon the word-level skip-gram model. However, while WL explicitly stores vectors for each word in the vocabulary, FT learns vector representations for character n-grams which appear within words. The embedding for an individual word is then identified with the sum of that word's n-gram vectors. As unseen words are still composed of familiar n-grams, this model is capable of assigning embedding vectors to words not seen in the training data. We used the fastText software package for this model[3].

2.3 Character-aware Skip-gram Model

Our character-aware skip-gram model (CL) models word meaning by learning representations for individual characters. It consists of two components: the *embedding subnet* generates embeddings for individual words using a convolutional neural network (CNN). The *NCE loss layer* uses a skip-gram loss function to score the embeddings. This architecture allows character-level sequence information to inform word embeddings, while using a loss function similar to those of more traditional embedding architectures.

Embedding Subnet. The *embedding subnet* is a CNN that takes as input a character sequence (representing a word), and outputs an embedding vector for that word. The architecture of this network was adapted from Kim et al. (2016), with modifications to use a skip-gram loss function and to produce low-dimensional embedding vectors.

Figure 1 provides a schematic overview of the embedding subnet. First, input words are normalized to a length of 16 characters, truncating longer words and appending null characters to the end of shorter ones. Each character in this input sequence is then assigned a character-embedding vector. The values of these character embeddings are trainable parameters of the model. The resulting sequence of character embeddings is then used as the input for a convolution layer, with a sigmoid activation function. A max-pooling layer is applied to all outputs of the convolution layer. The results of this pooling are all concatenated to form a single vector, which is then passed through two successive highway networks (Srivastava et al., 2015). Since highway networks preserve dimensionality,

---

[2] https://code.google.com/archive/p/word2vec/

[3] https://github.com/facebookresearch/fastText

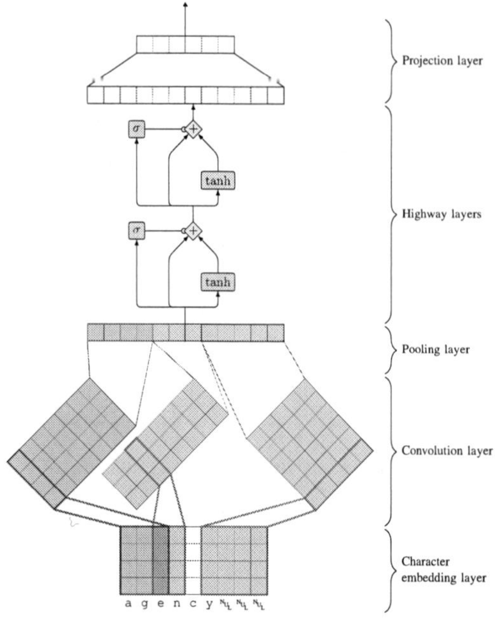

Figure 1: Embedding subnet

Corpus	Articles	Tokens	Vocab	Size
en-full	4,280,642	1,699M	8,745K	8.69 GiB
en-100M	48,430	19,211K	468K	100 MiB
en-10M	4,833	1,924K	106K	10.0 MiB
de-full	1,539,077	587M	6,323K	3.50 GiB
de-100M	43,078	16,507K	720K	100 MiB
de-10M	4,362	1,645K	153K	9.99 MiB

Table 2: Statistics for training corpora.

Benchmark	Mean Freq.	Morphemes per word	Portion OOV
WS353	44.7K	1.27	0/437
RW	1.91K	1.53	19/2951
WS353-de	8.36K	1.30	2/455
GUR350	3.11K	1.46	13/469

Table 3: Statistics for evaluation benchmarks (computed on full-size corpora). Frequencies averaged geometrically (on lemmas with non-zero frequency); morphemes/word averaged algebraically.

the output of the second highway network depends directly on the number of convolution filters used. As we would like a word embedding of relatively small dimensionality, we use a linear projection layer to yield our final embedding vector.

NCE Loss. In order for the embedding subnet to produce semantically-meaningful embeddings, we use it in a skip-gram model (Mikolov et al., 2013a) using noise-contrastive estimation (NCE) loss (Gutmann and Hyvärinen, 2012; Mnih and Teh, 2012). This is rather similar to the NEG models of Mikolov et al. (2013b), but with "input" vectors coming from our embedding subnet, and with NCE in the place of negative sampling. As in Mikolov et al. (2013b), we still depend on a fixed vocabulary of context words for the "output" vectors. All model parameters are optimized to minimize NCE loss using stochastic gradient descent.

2.4 Fusion model

CAT assigns each word the concatenation of its CL, WL, and FT embeddings, i.e., performs late fusion (Bruni et al., 2014). As the individual models produce vectors of different average magnitudes, we rescale the embeddings produced by individual models prior to this concatenation, such that, after rescaling, each constituent model has the same average vector magnitude, when averaged over all words present in the training data. Experiments

with joint training of the models did not yield superior results.

3 Experimental Setup

We evaluate our models for two languages, English and German. These are clearly not low-resource languages, but the availability of corpora and evaluation datasets makes them suitable for experiments.

Training data. All models were trained on the standard Wikipedia corpora for English and German preprocessed by Al-Rfou et al. (2013).[4]

In addition, we sampled two (sub)corpora with 10 and 100 million characters to evaluate the models' effectiveness on limited training data. To generate a subcorpus of a particular size, articles were sampled uniformly at random (without replacement) from that language's Wikipedia until the target size was reached. Table 2 presents all corpora and subcorpora used, and their sizes. Our 100M corpora account for around 1% (for English) and 3% (for German) of the full Wikipedia corpora, and 10M corpora for .1% and .3%, respectively. We picked these sizes because they cover the "typical" Wikipedia sizes for low-resource languages.

Evaluation benchmarks. We evaluate our models on a standard task in lexical semantics, predicting human word relatedness ratings. Compared to relation prediction, this task has the advantage of

---

[4]https://sites.google.com/site/rmyeid/projects/polyglot

Test	Benchmark	size	WL	FT	CL	CAT
all items	[en] WS353	353	.73	**.74**	.51	.72
	[en] RW	2034	.44	**.50**	.31	.46
	[de] WS353	350	**.64**	**.64**	.47	**.64**
	[de] GUR350	350	.61	**.72**	.52	.65
IV items	[en] WS353	353	**.73**	**.73**	.51	.72
	[en] RW	1977	.45	**.50**	.32	.47
	[de] WS353	348	**.64**	**.64**	.47	**.64**
	[de] GUR350	324	.64	**.72**	.55	.67
OOV items	[en] WS353	0	–	–	–	–
	[en] RW	57	-.24	**.64**	-.04	.15
	[de] WS353	2	**1.00**	**1.00**	-1.00	**1.00**
	[de] GUR350	26	-.11	**.61**	.00	.25

Table 4: Spearman correlations of embedding similarity and human judgments (full training sets: en 9G, de 3.5G). Top: full benchmarks; middle: in-vocabulary items; bottom: out-of-vocabulary items. Best model for each benchmark and training bolded.

Test	Benchmark	size	WL	FT	CL	CAT
all items	[en] WS353	353	.65	.66	.42	**.67**
	[en] RW	2034	.22	**.43**	.29	.40
	[de] WS353	350	.49	.50	.30	**.52**
	[de] GUR350	350	.32	**.56**	.51	.47
IV items	[en] WS353	353	.65	.66	.42	**.67**
	[en] RW	1413	.30	**.45**	.33	.42
	[de] WS353	347	.48	.49	.29	**.52**
	[de] GUR350	290	.42	**.55**	.52	.51
OOV items	[en] WS353	0	–	–	–	–
	[en] RW	621	.15	**.41**	.21	.35
	[de] WS353	3	.50	**1.00**	.50	.50
	[de] GUR350	60	.14	**.62**	.41	.41

Table 5: Spearman correlations of embedding similarity and human judgments (100M training sets).

Test	Benchmark	size	WL	FT	CL	CAT
all items	[en] WS353	353	.48	.42	.26	**.53**
	[en] RW	2034	.16	**.32**	.16	.28
	[de] WS353	350	.16	.22	.16	**.29**
	[de] GUR350	350	.11	.34	**.42**	.38
IV items	[en] WS353	333	.52	.44	.29	**.56**
	[en] RW	687	.21	**.34**	.16	.30
	[de] WS353	305	.16	.24	.21	**.28**
	[de] GUR350	218	.29	.40	.32	**.48**
OOV items	[en] WS353	20	**.52**	.05	-.05	.10
	[en] RW	1347	.19	**.30**	.16	.29
	[de] WS353	45	.16	.18	.18	**.24**
	[de] GUR350	132	.08	.25	**.40**	.31

Table 6: Spearman correlations of embedding similarity and human judgments (10M training sets).

being graded instead of categorical (Landauer and Dumais, 1997). We use two relatedness datasets in both languages. For comparison to prior work, and for a rough comparison across languages, we utilize the WordSim353 benchmark (WS353) (Finkelstein et al., 2001) for English and the German version of the Multilingual WordSim353 benchmark (WS353-de) for German (Leviant and Reichart, 2015).

As we are specifically interested in modeling rare words, we also use the Stanford Rare Word Dataset (RW, Luong et al. 2013) for English. It was designed with these goals in mind. While no parallel to this benchmark exists for German, the GUR350 benchmark (Zesch et al., 2007) shows similar properties: As Table 3 shows, the words in GUR350 are less frequent and longer than in WS353-de. Thus, many more words are out of vocabulary in GUR350 even in the full corpus.

4 Results

Tables 4 to 6 show the results for the three different training corpus sizes. We report results for all items, just in-vocabulary items, and just out-of-vocabulary items (i.e., one or both elements of the word pair unseen in training).

Full corpus results. The results by WL on full corpora for all items (top part of Table 4) outperform results reported in the literature[5], indicating that the word-level embeddings are competitive

with the state of the art. FT performs as well or even better than WL on the full corpora, indicating that character n-grams can learn well even from large datasets, while the individual character-based CL model cannot profit from this situation. Nevertheless, the fusion model CAT is robust: it performs generally on par with WL.

On full corpora, almost all items in all benchmark datasets are seen; therefore, the separate results on IV and OOV items are not particularly interesting (middle and bottom parts of Table 4).

100M corpora results. The results on the 100M corpora (Table 5) confirm that model performance correlates with training set size: Without exception, the models' performance decreases for smaller corpora. However, this effect is much more pronounced for WL than for the character-based models, FT and CL. For the first time, on these corpora, the fusion model CAT is able to outperform FT, indicating that there is some degree of complementarity between the predictions (and the errors) of

---

[5]For WordSim, Leviant and Reichart (2015) obtain 0.652 (en) and 0.618 (de) using our "full" corpora. For RW, Sahlgren and Lenci (2016) report 0.285 on 1G words, and for GUR350, Utt and Padó (2014) report 0.42 using 3G words.

the individual models.

On the 100M corpora, the RW and GUR350 datasets both have a significant number of pairs containing OOV words. As expected, WL performed particularly poorly on these pairs. However, it is notable that FT also outperforms WL on every IV benchmark. This shows that the advantage of character-based over word-based models is not restricted to unseen words. The performance gap between FT and WL on IV is small on the two WS353 datasets (with the highest mean item frequency, and the lowest morphological complexity – cf. Table 3) but substantial for RW and GUR350 (which contain low-frequency, morphologically complex words). This indicates that WL struggles in particular with infrequent, complex words.

10M corpora results. Finally, Table 6 shows the results for the 10M corpora. Here, we see a relatively heterogeneous picture regarding the individual models across benchmarks: WL does best on WS353-en; FT does best on RW and WS353-de; CL does best on GUR350. This behavior is consistent with the patterns we found for the 100M corpora, but more marked. Due to the inhomogeneity among models, the fusion model CAT does particularly well, outperforming FT on 3 of 4 benchmarks, often substantially so.

As with the 100M corpora, the character aware models perform much better than WL for OOV pairs. For 10M, however, FT's dominance is not as clear – CL substantially outperforms FT on GUR350. This may indicate that modeling individual character embeddings rather than n-grams is more suitable for the lowest-data setups.

Model choice recommendations. Based on our results, we can formulate the following recommendations: (a) FastText is a good choice for both medium- and large-data situations and is likely to outperform plain word-based models overall, and in particular for low-frequency words; (b) for low-data situations, there is sufficient complementarity among models that model combination, even by simple concatenation, can yield further substantial improvements.

5 Conclusion

This paper argues that it is worthwhile, both from applied and psycholinguistic perspectives, to evaluate embedding models trained on much smaller corpora than generally considered, and have compared a standard word-level skip-gram model against a character n-gram based and a single character-based embedding model.

Even at corpus sizes of billions of words, we find that the character n-gram based model performs at or above the level of the word-level model. This result is in contrast to the findings of Sahlgren and Lenci (2016), who found the best performance for a dimensionality-reduced word embedding model across all corpus sizes. However, all of the models they considered were word-based, indicating that character awareness is what makes the difference. The success of the character n-gram based model can also be interpreted as support for a morpheme-based representation in the mental lexicon (Smolka et al., 2014) in the sense that character n-gram appear to be represent a very informative level of representation for semantic information.

As we move to smaller corpus sizes, we also see more competitive performance for the model based on individual character embeddings. Its forte is to deal with low-data situations, predicting meanings for unfamiliar words by utilizing familiar morphemes and other subword structures, in line with Landauer et al.'s (1997) claim of "vast numbers of weak interrelations that, if properly exploited, can greatly amplify learning by a process of inference". In the future, we will evaluate our character-based model for other languages, and assess other aspects of its psycholinguistic plausibility, such as matching human behavior in performance and acquisition speed (Baroni et al., 2007).

Acknowledgments. Partial funding for this study was provided by Deutsche Forschungsgemeinschaft (project PA 1956/4-1).

References

Rami Al-Rfou, Bryan Perozzi, and Steven Skiena. 2013. Polyglot: Distributed word representations for multilingual NLP. In *Proceedings of CoNLL*. Sofia, Bulgaria, pages 183–192.

Marco Baroni, Alessandro Lenci, and Luca Onnis. 2007. Isa meets lara: An incremental word space model for cognitively plausible simulations of semantic learning. In *Proceedings of the ACL Workshop on Cognitive Aspects of Computational Language Acquisition*. Prague, Czech Republic, pages 49–56.

Piotr Bojanowski, Edouard Grave, Armand Joulin, and Tomas Mikolov. 2017. Enriching word vectors with subword information. *Transactions of the Association for Computational Linguistics* 5:135–146.

Elia Bruni, Nam Khanh Tran, and Marco Baroni. 2014. Multimodal distributional semantics. *Journal of Artificial Intelligence Research* 49:1–47.

Lev Finkelstein, Evgeniy Gabrilovich, Yossi Matias, Ehud Rivlin, Zach Solan, Gadi Wolfman, and Eytan Ruppin. 2001. Placing search in context: The concept revisited. In *Proceedings of WWW*. Hong Kong, China, pages 406–414.

Michael U Gutmann and Aapo Hyvärinen. 2012. Noise-contrastive estimation of unnormalized statistical models, with applications to natural image statistics. *Journal of Machine Learning Research* 13(Feb):307–361.

Yoon Kim, Yacine Jernite, David Sontag, and Alexander M Rush. 2016. Character-aware neural language models. In *Proceedings of AAAI*. Phoenix, AZ, pages 2741–2749.

Thomas K Landauer and Susan T Dumais. 1997. A solution to Plato's problem: The latent semantic analysis theory of acquisition, induction, and representation of knowledge. *Psychological Review* 104(2):211–240.

Ira Leviant and Roi Reichart. 2015. Separated by an un-common language: Towards judgment language informed vector space modeling. *arXiv preprint arXiv:1508.00106* .

Minh-Thang Luong, Richard Socher, and Christopher D Manning. 2013. Better word representations with recursive neural networks for morphology. In *Proceedings of CoNLL*. Sofia, Bulgaria, pages 104–113.

Tomas Mikolov, Kai Chen, Greg Corrado, and Jeffrey Dean. 2013a. Efficient estimation of word representations in vector space. *arXiv preprint arXiv:1301.3781* .

Tomas Mikolov, Ilya Sutskever, Kai Chen, Greg S Corrado, and Jeff Dean. 2013b. Distributed representations of words and phrases and their compositionality. In *Proceedings of NIPS*. pages 3111–3119.

Andriy Mnih and Yee Whye Teh. 2012. A fast and simple algorithm for training neural probabilistic language models. *arXiv preprint arXiv:1206.6426* .

Jeffrey Pennington, Richard Socher, and Christopher Manning. 2014. Glove: Global vectors for word representation. In *Proceedings of EMNLP*. Doha, Qatar, pages 1532–1543.

Magnus Sahlgren and Alessandro Lenci. 2016. The effects of data size and frequency range on distributional semantic models. In *Proceedings of EMNLP*. Austin, TX, pages 975–980.

Eva Smolka, Katrin H. Preller, and Carsten Eulitz. 2014. 'verstehen' ('understand') primes 'stehen' ('stand'): Morphological structure overrides semantic compositionality in the lexical representation of german complex verbs. *Journal of Memory and Language* 72:16–36.

Rupesh Kumar Srivastava, Klaus Greff, and Jürgen Schmidhuber. 2015. Highway networks. *arXiv preprint arXiv:1505.00387* .

Jason Utt and Sebastian Padó. 2014. Crosslingual and multilingual construction of syntax-based vector space models. *Transactions of the Association of Computational Linguistics* 2:245–258.

Torsten Zesch, Iryna Gurevych, and Max Mühlhäuser. 2007. Comparing Wikipedia and German Wordnet by evaluating semantic relatedness on multiple datasets. In *Proceedings of NAACL-HLT*. Rochester, NY, pages 205–208.

Subword-level Composition Functions for Learning Word Embeddings

Bofang Li[1], **Aleksandr Drozd**[2], **Tao Liu**[3], and **Xiaoyong Du**[4]

[1,2]School of Computing, Department of Mathematical and Computing Science,
Tokyo Institute of Technology, Tokyo, Japan
[1,3,4]School of Information, Renmin University of China, Beijing, China
[1,3,4]Key laboratory of Data Engineering and Knowledge Engineering, MOE, Beijing, China
[1]libofang@ruc.edu.cn
[2]alex@smg.is.titech.ac.jp
[3]tliu@ruc.edu.cn
[4]duyong@ruc.edu.cn

Abstract

Subword-level information is crucial for capturing the meaning and morphology of words, especially for out-of-vocabulary entries. We propose CNN- and RNN-based subword-level composition functions for learning word embeddings, and systematically compare them with popular word-level and subword-level models (Skip-Gram and FastText). Additionally, we propose a hybrid training scheme in which a pure subword-level model is trained jointly with a conventional word-level embedding model based on lookup-tables. This increases the fitness of all types of subword-level word embeddings; the word-level embeddings can be discarded after training, leaving only compact subword-level representation with much smaller data volume. We evaluate these embeddings on a set of intrinsic and extrinsic tasks, showing that subword-level models have advantage on tasks related to morphology and datasets with high OOV rate, and can be combined with other types of embeddings.

1 Introduction

Word embeddings are used in many natural language processing tasks (Collobert et al., 2011; Socher et al., 2013; Kim, 2014). In word embedding models, words are mapped or "embedded" into low-dimensional real-valued vectors. Such mapping is based, implicitly or explicitly, on word co-occurrence statistics (Levy and Goldberg, 2014b).

Naturally, frequent words provide a better representation of their distributional properties; thus the quality of word embeddings is in direct relation to the frequency of words (Drozd et al., 2015). However, even in large corpora, most words occur very few times. For example, Baroni (2009) shows that the words occurring 3 times or less constitute almost 70% of the vocabulary. Consequently, most of the in-vocabulary words (for a given task/corpora) have to be discarded or embedded into low-quality vectors. Therefore, word-level models suffer from data sparsity.

Another issue with word-level models is that they do not make use of morphological information. Different forms of the same word are treated as completely unrelated entities. For example, as shown in Section 4.2, we find that the word "physicist" and "physicists" are not close to each other in a well-know word embedding model Skip-Gram (Mikolov et al., 2013).

These two issues are addressed by the emerging methodology of subword-level representations, as discussed in Section 2. The most notable example of such representations is FastText (Bojanowski et al., 2017). It represents each word as a bag-of-character n-grams. Representations for character n-grams, once they are learned, can be combined (via simple summation) to represent out-of-vocabulary (OOV) words.

This paper contributes to the discussion of composition functions for constructing subword-level embeddings and their evaluation. We propose and evaluate several models (including convolutional and recurrent neural networks) that can embed arbitrary character sequences into vectors. Our models do not rely on any external resource. We also propose a hybrid training scheme, which

Proceedings of the Second Workshop on Subword/Character LEvel Models, pages 38–48
New Orleans, Louisiana, June 6, 2018. ©2018 Association for Computational Linguistics

makes these neural networks directly integrated into Skip-Gram model. We train two sets of word embeddings simultaneously: one is from a lookup table as in traditional Skip-Gram, and another is from convolutional or recurrent neural network. The former is better at capturing semantic similarity. The latter is more focused on morphology and can learn embeddings for OOV words. We conduct experiments on five tasks, and compare our models with original Skip-Gram and the state-of-the-art performer FastText.

2 Related Work

2.1 Morphology-based Models

Morphology has long been considered as an important feature for word representations. For example, Lazaridou et al. (2013) investigate several algebraic composition functions (e.g. addition or multiplication) for morphologically complex words, which generate better representations compared to traditional distributional semantic models. Luong et al. (2013) train a recursive neural network for morphological composition, and show its effectiveness on (rare) word similarity task. Qiu et al. (2014) propose Morpheme CBOWs for word similarity and word analogy tasks, which improves on CBOW model (Mikolov et al., 2013) by learning morphology embeddings and word embeddings simultaneously. Alexandrescu and Kirchhoff (2006) take morphological tags as features (one-hot representation) for training a language model, which reduce the perplexity on rare word language modeling scenarios.

For both language modeling and machine translation tasks, LBL++ Botha and Blunsom (2014) show the effectiveness of summing morphology vectors in log-bilinear model (Mnih and Hinton, 2007) on 6 morphologically rich languages. Similarly, Morph-LBL (Cotterell and Schütze, 2015) improves on LBL model by predicting both context words and words' morphological tags in a semi-supervised fashion, which outperforms both Word2Vec and LBL on German morphological analysis.

However, all the above models rely on prior morphological knowledge, which is obtained by morphology analysis tools such as Morfessor (Creutz and Lagus, 2007), or an annotated morphology corpus such as CELEX (Baayen et al., 1995) and TIGER (Brants et al., 2004).

2.2 Subword-level Word Embeddings

Another line of work is focused on end-to-end word embedding learning based on subword-level information. FastText (Bojanowski et al., 2017) is probably the most influential and effective recent model. It represents each word as a bag-of-character n-grams. The models proposed in this paper are conceptually derived from FastText, i.e. we also operate on character n-grams level and predict context words from the target word, as in Skip-Gram approach.

Similarly to our proposed RNN, Cao and Rei (2016) train a bi-directional LSTM based on subword information. Instead of using character ngrams, their model feeds the word's prefixes and suffixes into each direction of LSTM respectively. This model is mainly designed to solve morphological boundary recovery task, it performs comparably with dedicated morphological analyzers. Pinter et al. (2017) also utilize BiLSTM to construct word embeddings. However, their model relies on pre-trained word embeddings by minimizing the squared Euclidean distance. In contrast, our proposed RNN requires only a plain text corpus.

2.3 Other Subword-level Models

There are also various task-specific NLP models that utilize character-level information for training deep neural networks in an end-to-end fashion. They often surpass the word-level baselines on language modeling (Mikolov et al., 2012; Sperr et al., 2013; Bojanowski et al., 2015; Kim et al., 2016), part-of-speech tagging (Ling et al., 2015; dos Santos and Zadrozny, 2014), text classification (Zhang et al., 2015), and machine translation (Sennrich et al., 2016; Luong and Manning, 2016), etc. However, these models do not produce representations that could be used in other tasks.

3 Models

3.1 Skip-Gram

Due to its popularity, simplicity, and state-of-the-art performance on a range of linguistic tasks, Skip-Gram (Mikolov et al., 2013) has been widely used as baseline in the word embedding literature (Levy and Goldberg, 2014a; Faruqui et al., 2015; Bojanowski et al., 2017; Zhao et al., 2017). In particular, we use Skip-Gram with negative sampling technique (Figure 1-a). For a vocabulary V of size $|V|$, Skip-Gram learns two set of vectors

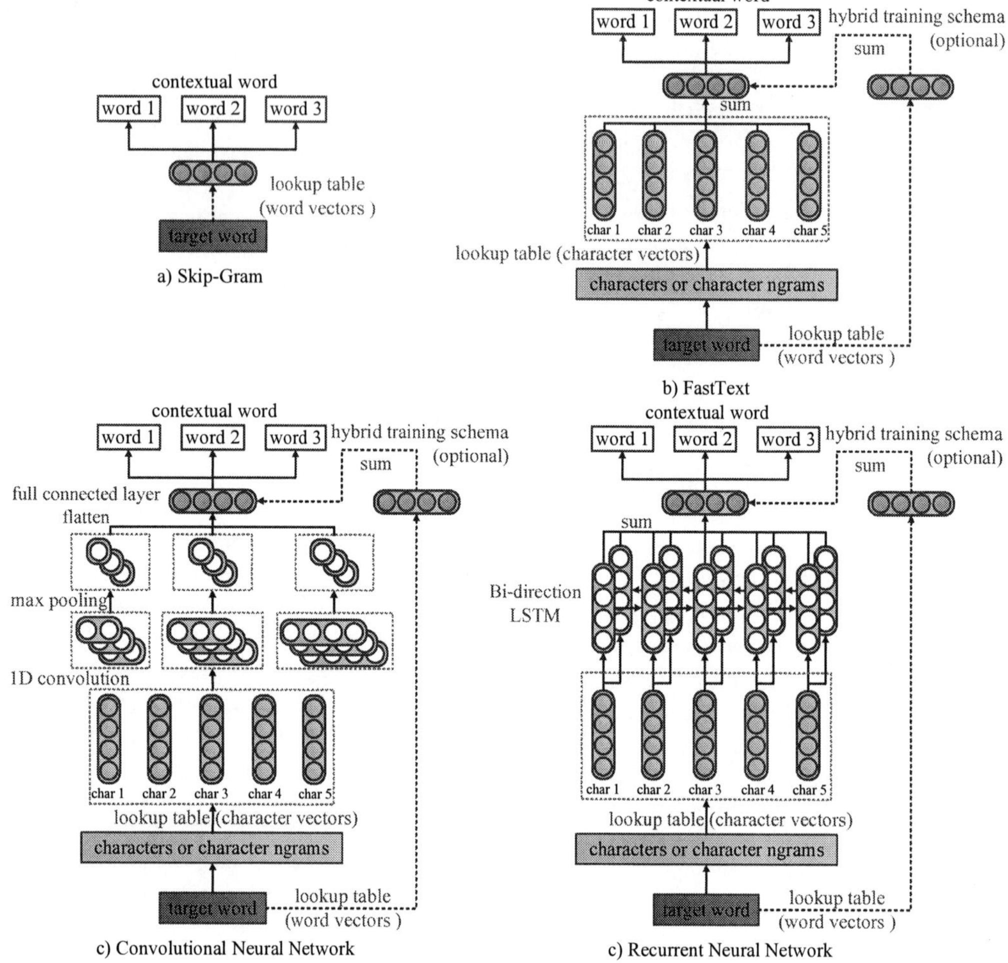

Figure 1: Illustration of original Skip-Gram and subword-level models.

$W, C \in \mathbb{R}^{|V|*N}$, namely word vectors and contextual word vectors. N is the dimension of vectors. Given a training corpus, Skip-Gram iterates through all words w and their contexts c, and maximizes the objective function $p(c|\vec{w})$, which is defined as:

$$\log \sigma\left(\vec{w} \cdot \vec{c}\right) + \sum_{k=1}^{K} \mathbb{E}_{c_i \sim \mathcal{N}_{w,c}} \left[\log \sigma\left(-\vec{w} \cdot \vec{c_i}\right)\right] \tag{1}$$

where σ is the sigmoid function. $\vec{w} \in W$ and $\vec{c} \in C$ are the vectors for word w and context c respectively. K is the negative sampling size. $\mathcal{N}_{w,c}$ is the negative example that sampled from the vocabulary V. The negative sampling probability is empirically defined as the unigram probability of a word raised to the power of $3/4$.

3.2 Utilizing Subword Information

In order to make use of subword information, we first generalize the objective function of Skip-Gram by replacing word vector $\vec{w}$ with a composition function $f(w)$. $f(w)$ takes word w as an input and outputs a vector of length N. Overall, the objective function of generalized Skip-Gram is defined as:

$$p(c|f(w)) = \log \sigma\left(f(w) \cdot \vec{c}\right) \\ + \sum_{k=1}^{K} \mathbb{E}_{c_i \sim \mathcal{N}_{w,c}} \left[\log \sigma\left(-f(w) \cdot \vec{c_i}\right)\right] \tag{2}$$

In the original Skip-Gram model, the function

$f(w)$ is simply a lookup table, which projects word w to its corresponding vector $\vec{w}$ in the table. Depending on the definition, $f(w)$ could also take the subword information of w into consideration. Naturally, composition functions, especially neural networks, can be considered.

3.2.1 A Hybrid Training scheme for Subword-level Models

Intuitively, compared to Skip-Gram, subword-level models should be better suited for capturing morphology instead of similarity. In order to take advantage of both representations, we incorporate Skip-Gram into subword-level models. Formally, in our hybrid training scheme we define the objective function of subword-level models as:

$$p(c|\vec{w} + f(w)) \qquad (3)$$

In this case, each word will have two embeddings: one from the lookup table (the same as Skip-Gram), and another from the composition function f. These two types of embeddings are learned simultaneously. We denote the embedding model from the word-level lookup table as Model_{word}, and the one from composition function as $\text{Model}_{subword}$. As a baseline we additionally train embeddings using only subword-level composition function; these models will be referred to as $\text{Model}_{vanilla}$.

3.2.2 FastText (Summation)

Probably the most simple and intuitive way of utilizing subword information is to sum all vectors of characters and character ngrams belonging to a word (Figure 1-b), which is pioneered by Bojanowski et al. (2017). Formally, the composition function is defined as $f(w) = \sum_{g \in \mathcal{G}_w} \vec{g}$, where g is the character n-gram, and $\vec{g}$ is its corresponding n-gram vector with length N. $\mathcal{G}_w$ is the set of character n-grams for word w. For example, when $n = 3$, $\mathcal{G}_w$ for word "bigger" is defined as `<bi, big, igg, gge, ger, er>`. The angle brackets are padding at the start and end of the word.

Note that the original FastText ($\text{FastText}_{vanilla}$) does not have the hybrid training scheme. As later shown in our experiments, FastText_{word} from the hybrid training scheme works better than $\text{FastText}_{vanilla}$ in some semantic relatedness datasets. Moreover, hybrid training scheme is essential for other types of composition functions.

For fair comparison, in the following models, we use the same padding and the same length of character n-grams' vector.

3.2.3 Convolutional Neural Network

Despite its simplicity and efficiency, there is no clear evidence that simple summation as in FastText is the best choice for composing subword information.

This paper investigate two neural network. We first consider the Convolutional Neural Network (CNN) as composition function $f(w)$. CNN (LeCun, 1998) is able to capture local features automatically, and has been applied to a wide range of NLP tasks (Kim et al., 2016; Zhang et al., 2015; Luong and Manning, 2016).

The CNN architecture introduced in this paper is inspired by the model used for language modeling in Kim et al. (2016). As illustrated in Figure 1-c, similarly to FastText, the vectors of characters are first extracted from a lookup table. Those vectors form a matrix with size $N * L$, where L is the number of characters. The 1D convolution filters are used to extract local features. We apply 1D convolutions of size ranging from 1 to 7 in parallel, perform max-pooling and concatenate the output. Each of the convolutions uses 200 filters. The output of this model is a fully-connected layer with the number of units corresponding to the desired size of embeddings. The resulting vector is used for predicting contextual words using negative sampling, the same as the negative sampling in Skip-Gram.

3.2.4 Recurrent Neural Network

Another neural network that is worth considering is Recurrent Neural Network (RNN). It takes a sequence of arbitrary length as an input, and outputs a vector that represents this sequence. Among all the different variations, the Long Short-Term Memory based recurrent neural network (LSTM) (Hochreiter and Schmidhuber, 1997) and its bi-direction version (Schuster and Paliwal, 1997) are easier to train, and better capture long-distance information. As illustrated in Figure 1-d, for each direction, an LSTM runs over all the vectors of characters in the word w. The hidden layers at each position are then summed together, and the resulting vector is fed into a fully connected layer to form the final vector w. We empirically set the hidden layer size of LSTM to $N * 2$.

Skip-Gram	FastText$_{subword}$	RNN$_{subword}$	CNN$_{subword}$
geneticists cosmologists	musicologists classicists	psychologists **physiologist**	protists **physicians**
logicians historians	biophysicist **physicians**	trombonists pharmacists	cryonicists **physician**
humanists geographers	**physicalism physicist**	aerodynamicists **physiocrats**	artists **physicality**
zoologists philosophers	mathematicians publicists	**physicist** microeconomists	**physiocrats** publicists
astrologers astronomers	ethicists eugenicists	**physicality physicians**	**physics physicist**

Table 1: Illustration of the top-10 most similar words of target word "physicists".

4 Experiments

4.1 Implementation Details

We implemented all models described in section 3 using Chainer deep learning framework (Tokui et al., 2015). Since the proposed CNN and RNN architectures significantly increase computational requirements for training, we choose a relatively small TEXT8[1] corpus for this evaluation. This corpus contains the first 10^9 bytes of the English Wikipedia dump from Mar. 3, 2006. The word embedding size N is set to 300. The batch size is fixed to 1000. The negative sampling size is set to 5, and the window size is set to 2. Following Chainer's original word2vec implementation, we use Adam (Kingma and Ba, 2014) as the optimization function. Words which appear fewer than five times are directly discarded, which results in vocabulary size of 71290. For character ngrams, we follow the FastText's best configuration and use 5-grams for FastText. We also discard character ngrams which appear fewer than five times, which results in character ngrams vocabulary size of 143207. Word embedding models are trained for 5 epochs on Nvidia Tesla K80 or P100 GPU.

We also download the state-of-the-art FastText embeddings (denoted as FastText$_{external}$)[2], which are trained on a much larger full Wikipedia corpus. Note that since CNN and RNN require approximate 45 and 65 days of training on K80, we didn't train on this corpus.

For the fair comparison, we ensure that all embeddings used in evaluations use exactly same vocabulary. Unlike most of the benchmarks, where only embeddings of encountered words affect resulting accuracy, analogical reasoning benchmark is sensitive to the entire vocabulary in terms of size and embeddings of individual words. For example it is hard to make a mistake when looking for "Paris" as the pair for "France" if the whole vocabulary contains only these two words. Furthermore, accuracy depends on how close the target word is to the source words (Rogers et al., 2017), which could also be affected by a larger vocabulary.

This issue is especially pronounced for embeddings with dynamic vocabulary, such as subword-level models evaluated in this study. In our pilot experiments, models with large vocabulary like FastText$_{external}$ result in poor performance on word analogy tasks since large vocabulary increases the number of options.

Skip-Gram	FastText$_{vanilla}$	FastText$_{external}$
85.6M	171.9M	8493.6M

CNN$_{vanilla}$	RNN$_{vanilla}$	
7.5M	19.1M	

Table 2: Memory footprint of different models (For Skip-Gram and FastText, it will increase on larger vocabulary. For CNN- and RNN-based models, it is constant.

Note that the sizes of these models are different, as shown in Table 2. Due to the large number of character ngrams, FastText requires the most data among these models, while CNN needs only a few megabytes of data.

4.2 Qualitative Analysis

Before looking into the performance of models on specific tasks, we first conduct qualitative analysis. We choose several target words and analyze their nearest neighbors in Skip-Gram, FastText$_{subword}$, CNN$_{subword}$, and RNN$_{subword}$. We find that subword-level models, especially CNN- and RNN-based models, tend to cluster words with the same morpheme together. Taking target word "physicists" as an example (Table 1), the word "physicist" is within the top-10 nearest neighbors in subword-level models, but not in

---

[1] http://mattmahoney.net/dc/textdata.html

[2] https://github.com/facebookresearch/fastText

Model	Rare Words	WS sem.	WS rel.	Sim 999	MEN	Mech Turk	BATS inf.	BATS der.	BATS enc.	BATS lex.	Google sem.	Google syn.
		Word Similarity					Word Analogy					
Skip-Gram	.059	.658	.586	.285	.555	.577	.652	.096	.280	.098	**.427**	.534
FastText$_{word}$	.065	.708	**.619**	.285	.610	.596	.622	.102	.274	.078	.424	.530
CNN$_{word}$	.058	.670	.584	.245	.554	.584	.628	.108	.250	.074	.416	.489
LSTM$_{word}$	.063	.697	.623	.284	.600	.599	.666	.134	.264	.080	.427	.597
Concat$_{word}$							.712	.184	.316	**.130**	.492	.649
FastText$_{subword}$	.085	.707	.566	.273	.620	.582	.790	.580	**.290**	.082	.374	**.812**
CNN$_{subword}$	.051	.581	.417	.190	.478	.509	.758	.682	.076	.028	.019	.789
RNN$_{subword}$	.063	.664	.532	.282	.566	.579	.798	.672	.114	.028	.061	.786
Concat$_{subword}$							.846	.696	.326	.078	.290	.914
FastText$_{word+subword}$							.792	.578	**.350**	.104	**.439**	.856
CNN$_{word+subword}$							.832	.638	.242	.084	.160	.859
RNN$_{word+subword}$							.832	.606	.244	.086	.240	.875
FastText$_{subword+OOV}$	.344	.715	.575	.277	.619	.599	.842	.824	.254	.096	.340	.776
CNN$_{subword+OOV}$	.234	.564	.409	.224	.490	.497	.880	**.948**	.094	.044	.023	.786
RNN$_{subword+OOV}$	.299	.670	.540	**.286**	.566	.587	**.908**	.906	.134	.040	.061	.796
Concat$_{subword+OOV}$							**.962**	**.960**	.328	.116	.298	**.917**
FastText$_{vanilla+OOV}$	.348	.717	.579	.283	.630	.624	.840	.834	.252	**.116**	.347	.799
CNN$_{vanilla+OOV}$	.212	.535	.400	.185	.474	.556	.874	.918	.104	.042	.015	.773
RNN$_{vanilla+OOV}$	.273	.638	.542	.250	.576	.568	.856	.866	.112	.034	.050	.748
Concat$_{vanilla+OOV}$							.958	.958	.314	.126	.275	.895
FastText$_{external}$	.096	.674	.604	.332	.600	.574	.746	.446	.528	.194	.779	.872
FastText$_{external+OOV}$	.431	.682	.607	.341	.600	.587	.834	.672	.562	.214	.798	.879

Table 3: Results on word similarity and word analogy datasets. For hybrid training scheme, we denote the embeddings that come from word vector lookup table as "Model$_{word}$", and the embeddings which come from the composition function as "Model$_{subword}$". We denote the vanilla (non-hybrid) models as "Model$_{vanilla}$". The "FastText$_{external}$" is the public available FastText embeddings, which are trained on the full Wikipedia corpus. We also test the version where OOV words are expanded, and denote as "Model$_{+OOV}$". Model combinations are denoted as gray rows, and best results among them are marked **bold**. Rare words dataset in blue column have 43.3% OOV rate, while other word similarity datasets have maximum 4.6% OOV rate. Morphology related categories are denoted as almond columns. The results of model combination for word similarity task are simply the average of results from each single models, which are not listed in this table.

Skip-Gram. Moreover, subword models tend to cluster words with the same morphology form (affix) together, especially for RNN and CNN.

4.3 Quantitative Analysis

4.3.1 Word Similarity

Word similarity task aims at producing semantic similarity scores of word pairs, which are compared with the human scores using Spearman's correlation. The cosine distance is used for generating similarity scores between two word vectors. In order to test the effectiveness of capturing word similarity for rare word, we choose the Rare Words dataset (Luong et al., 2013). For systematical comparison, we also test our models on the WordSim353 (WS) (Finkelstein et al., 2001) dataset, divided into similarity (sem.) and relatedness (rel.) categories (Zesch et al., 2008; Agirre et al., 2009), Sim 999 dataset (Hill et al., 2016), MEN dataset (Bruni et al., 2012), and Mech Turk dataset (Radinsky et al., 2011).

Table 3 shows that on word similarity tasks FastText models perform the best in all datasets except Sim 999. CNN$_{subword}$ and RNN$_{subword}$ are more focused on word morphology, and thus do not perform well on word similarity task.

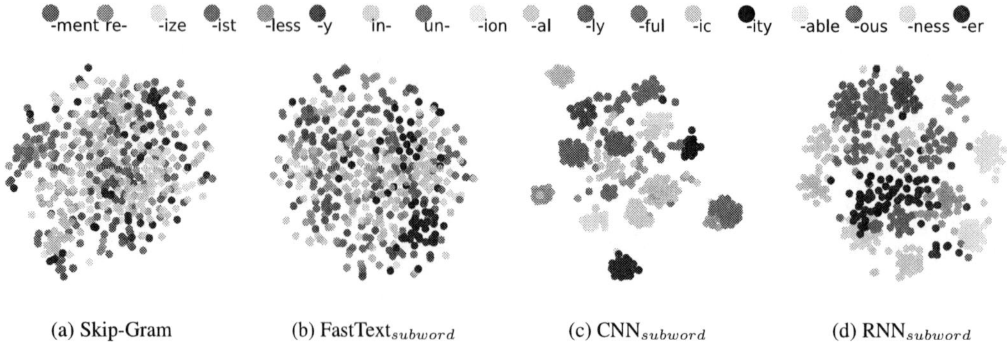

(a) Skip-Gram	(b) FastText$_{subword}$	(c) CNN$_{subword}$	(d) RNN$_{subword}$

Figure 3: Visualization of learned word embeddings, each dot represents a word, different colors represent different affixes.

However, compared to Skip-Gram, CNN$_{word}$ and RNN$_{word}$ (the versions with word vector lookup table) achieve comparable or even better results. Their word vector lookup tables in these models are affected by the composition function, which results in better performance.

Note that the Rare Words dataset has 43.3% of words which are OOV. In this dataset, the vocabulary expanded models (FastText$_{subword+OOV}$, CNN$_{subword+OOV}$, and RNN$_{subword+OOV}$) perform a lot better than others. This highlights the necessity of expanding vocabulary and the effectiveness of subword-level models.

4.3.2 Word Analogy

The word analogy task aims at answering questions generalize as "a is to a' as b is to __ ?", such as "London is to Britain as Tokyo is to Japan". We follow the evaluation protocol by Drozd et al. (2016) who proposed the LRCos method of solving word analogies, which significantly improves on the traditional vector offset method. We use Google analogy dataset (Mikolov et al., 2013) along with a much bigger and balanced BATS analogy dataset (Gladkova et al., 2016).

On word analogy datasets (Table 3), the inflectional and derivational morphology categories demonstrate the effectiveness of subword-level word models. It is especially obvious on derivation morphology category, where Skip-Gram only achieves 9.6% accuracy and subword-level models achieve minimal 57.8% accuracy (excluding the lookup table versions). Furthermore, when the vocabulary is expanded, the minimal accuracy of subword-level models reaches 82.4%.

Morphology-related analogy questions also benefit a lot from the model combination. No-

tably, Concat$_{subowrd+OOV}$ achieves an accuracy of 96.2% and 96.0% on inflection and derivation morphology, which is by far the highest accuracies on this two categories. We also observe that CNN is less sensitive to semantic word analogy, while performing the best on derivational word analogy.

4.3.3 Affix Prediction

In this section we test the ability of subword-level embeddings to predict what affix is present in a morphologically complex word. We use the dataset gathered by (Lazaridou et al., 2013), which contains 6549 stems and derived word pairs, such as "name"-"rename" and "sparse"-"sparsity". There are 18 affixes, such as "re-" and "-ity", and the task is to predict which one is present in a given word. We use the embeddings of derived words as input, and feed them to a logistic regression classifier for predicting their affixes. The accuracy, recall, and F_1-score are used for measurement. We also follow Lazaridou et al. (2013) in using the default training/test data split.

Figure 3 shows a t-SNE projection of the words with different affixes in the dataset. It is clear that both CNN and RNN are able to distinguish different derivation types, with the advantage of the former. This also confirms the good performance of CNN on derivational analogy task. Note that Fast-Text does not fare much better than Skip-Gram, although it is a subword-level model. This partially explains its low accuracy compared to other subword-level models on morphological analogy categories.

The prediction results in Table 4 reflect the cluster visualization in Figure 3. Moreover, as in the word analogy task, the concatenation (especially with the expanded vocabulary version) performs

Model	AP			SL		
	P	R	F_1	POS	Chunk	NER
Skip-Gram	.324	.270	.251	.878	.881	.915
FastText$_{word}$	.346	.267	.250	.880	.883	.917
CNN$_{word}$	.344	.289	.270	.877	.882	.912
LSTM$_{word}$	.354	.298	.280	.878	.882	.915
Concat$_{word}$	.359	.301	.298	.890	.891	.921
FastText$_{subword}$	.527	.430	.433	.830	.822	.910
CNN$_{subword}$	.878	.622	.694	.845	.850	.870
RNN$_{subword}$	.864	.614	.684	.866	.872	.897
Concat$_{subword}$	.900	.628	.705	.892	.890	.919
FastText$_{word+subword}$	.520	.426	.428	.886	.887	.920
CNN$_{word+subword}$	.886	.621	.696	.890	.888	.913
RNN$_{word+subword}$	.839	.607	.670	.890	.888	.919
FastText$_{subword+OOV}$	.564	.481	.493	.834	.804	**.929**
CNN$_{subword+OOV}$	.912	**.687**	.765	.909	.895	.909
RNN$_{subword+OOV}$	.890	.674	.751	.925	**.912**	<u>**.929**</u>
Concat$_{subword+OOV}$	<u>**.928**</u>	.694	<u>**.777**</u>	<u>**.945**</u>	.925	<u>**.948**</u>
FastText$_{vanilla+OOV}$	.574	.489	.502	.833	.803	<u>.929</u>
CNN$_{vanilla+OOV}$	<u>.920</u>	.689	.770	.907	.894	.906
RNN$_{vanilla+OOV}$	.897	.683	**.757**	.924	<u>.912</u>	.926
Concat$_{vanilla+OOV}$	.914	<u>**.701**</u>	.768	<u>**.945**</u>	<u>**.926**</u>	<u>**.948**</u>
FastText$_{external}$	.521	.411	.414	.888	.882	.929
FastText$_{external}$	.636	.707	.659	.941	.919	.940

Table 4: Results on affix prediction (AP) and sequence labeling (SL) tasks. Sequence labeling tasks have 16.5%, 27.1%, 28.5% OOV rate respectively.

the best among all the other models.

4.3.4 Sequence Labeling

Sequence labeling task consists in assigning labels to elements of texts. We evaluate word embedding models on Part-of-Speech Tagging (POS), Chunking[3] and Named Entity Recognition (NER) tasks [4]. Following the evaluation protocol used in Kiros et al. (2015); Li et al. (2017), we restrict the predicting model to Logistic Regression Classifier [5]. The classifier's input for predicting the label of word w_i is simply the concatenation of word vectors $\vec{w_{i-2}}, \vec{w_{i-1}}, \vec{w_i}, \vec{w_{i+1}}, \vec{w_{i+2}}$. This ensures that the quality of the embedding models is directly evaluated, and their strengths and weaknesses are easily observed.

Subword-level models on sequence labeling tasks clearly demonstrate the effectiveness of expanding OOV words. As shown in Table 4, expanding vocabulary boosts the performance by a large margin. For example, on NER task, FastText$_{subword+OOV}$, CNN$_{subword+OOV}$, and RNN$_{subword+OOV}$ achieve 1.9%, 2.1%, 3.2% absolute gains over the versions of the same models without expanded vocabulary.

4.3.5 Text Classification

For text classification task, we choose the movie review sentiment (MR) (Pang and Lee, 2005), customer product reviews (CR) (Nakagawa et al., 2010), subjectivity/objectivity classification (SUBJ) (Pang and Lee, 2004), and IMDB movie review (IMDB) (Maas et al., 2011) datasets. The classification is performed by Logistic Regression Classifier. The input of this classifier is the sum of word embeddings that belonging to the text.

As shown in Table 5, the input word embeddings do not considerably affect the final accuracy. This is especially obvious when comparing *subword* and *subword + OOV* models. It's hard to draw any insightful conclusion from this experiment. This is in line with the observations

---

[3]CoNLL 2000 shared task `http://www.cnts.ua.ac.be/conll2000/chunking`

[4]CoNLL 2003 shared task `http://www.cnts.ua.ac.be/conll2003/ner`

[5]`http://scikit-learn.org/`

of Li et al. (2017), who showed that Skip-Gram, CBOW, and GloVe trained with different context types perform similarly on text classification task.

5 Discussion

The evaluation showed that despite being trained on a relatively small corpus, CNN- and RNN-based (model-based) approaches outperform conventional (trained on word-level) embeddings as well as FastText embeddings, which are claimed to better capture morphological information (Bojanowski et al., 2017). In some cases, the performance of model-based embeddings is even higher than that of FastText embeddings that were trained on much larger corpus.

Moreover, such performance is achieved with very compact representations: it is possible to generate an embedding for any given word on demand with only network weights, and these weights require an order of mere kilobytes of data (Table 2). Naturally, these compact representations do not have enough capacity to capture semantic information well. However, besides merely indicating a possibility for improvement/limitations of more "heavy-weight" models (like original Skip-Gram or FastText), model-based embeddings can be used together with other approaches to improve their sensitivity to morphological information.

One such approach is to combine embeddings from different models after training, as demonstrated in our experiments ("concat" lines in Table 3). Simple concatenation of lookup-table-based and model-based embeddings maintain high accuracy on morphology-related benchmarks, while elevating performance on semantic tasks to comparable level.

Additionally, subword-level models can be trained *jointly* with models based on lookup-tables, which improves their performance on different tasks. After training, either part can be used independently or jointly (e.g. by concatenation) in down-stream tasks.

6 Conclusion

We have implemented and evaluated several types of composition functions for subword-level elements (characters and character n-grams) in the context of training word embeddings in Skip-Gram-like model.

We have shown that morphological information can be captured efficiently by extremely compact

Model	Text Classification			
	MR	CR	SUBJ	IMDB
Skip-Gram	.688	.765	.881	.797
FastText$_{word}$	.690	.756	.878	.796
CNN$_{word}$	.690	.764	.876	.796
LSTM$_{word}$	.687	.752	.881	.794
FastText$_{subword}$	.691	.758	.867	.798
CNN$_{subword}$	.670	.759	.857	.784
RNN$_{subword}$	.689	.758	.872	.796
FastText$_{subword+OOV}$	.693	.759	.869	.797
CNN$_{subword+OOV}$	.675	.763	.858	.785
RNN$_{subword+OOV}$	.692	.760	.872	.795
FastText$_{word+subword}$	.693	.759	.869	.797
CNN$_{word+subword}$	.675	.763	.858	.785
RNN$_{word+subword}$	.692	.760	.872	.795

Table 5: Results on text classification datasets.

models. Embeddings generated dynamically from just a few megabytes of parameters significantly outperform conventional (word2vec and FastText) models on morphology related tasks. Additionally, this indicates the vast limitation of the ability of conventional models to capture morphological information.

To model both morphological and semantic information, we propose two methods for combining strength of compact subword-level- and lookup-table based models: merging trained embeddings and training jointly. The resulting embeddings achieved high accuracy on a range of benchmarks and are particularly promising for datasets with high OOV rate.

The source code of those models, along with the pretrained word embeddings, has been integrated into an open-source project, and will be publicly available.

Acknowledgments

This work was partially supported by JSPS KAKENHI Grant No. JP17K12739, JST CREST Grant No. JPMJCR1687 and National Natural Science Foundation of China Grant No.61472428.

References

Eneko Agirre, Enrique Alfonseca, Keith Hall, Jana Kravalova, Marius Paşca, and Aitor Soroa. 2009. A study on similarity and relatedness using distributional and wordnet-based approaches. In *NAACL*, pages 19–27. Association for Computational Linguistics.

Andrei Alexandrescu and Katrin Kirchhoff. 2006. Factored neural language models. In *HLT-NAACL*.

R Harald Baayen, Richard Piepenbrock, and Leon Gulikers. 1995. The celex lexical database (release 2). *Distributed by the Linguistic Data Consortium, University of Pennsylvania.*

Marco Baroni. 2009. Distributions in text.

Piotr Bojanowski, Edouard Grave, Armand Joulin, and Tomas Mikolov. 2017. Enriching word vectors with subword information. *Transactions of the Association for Computational Linguistics*, 5:135–146.

Piotr Bojanowski, Armand Joulin, and Tomas Mikolov. 2015. Alternative structures for character-level rnns. *CoRR*, abs/1511.06303.

Jan A. Botha and Phil Blunsom. 2014. Compositional morphology for word representations and language modelling. In *ICML*.

Sabine Brants, Stefanie Dipper, Peter Eisenberg, Silvia Hansen-Schirra, Esther König, Wolfgang Lezius, Christian Rohrer, George Smith, and Hans Uszkoreit. 2004. Tiger: Linguistic interpretation of a german corpus. *Research on language and computation*, 2(4):597–620.

Elia Bruni, Gemma Boleda, Marco Baroni, and Nam-Khanh Tran. 2012. Distributional semantics in technicolor. In *ACL*, pages 136–145. Association for Computational Linguistics.

Kris Cao and Marek Rei. 2016. A joint model for word embedding and word morphology. *ACL 2016*, page 18.

Ronan Collobert, Jason Weston, Léon Bottou, Michael Karlen, Koray Kavukcuoglu, and Pavel Kuksa. 2011. Natural language processing (almost) from scratch. *The Journal of Machine Learning Research*, 12:2493–2537.

Ryan Cotterell and Hinrich Schütze. 2015. Morphological word-embeddings. In *HLT-NAACL*, pages 1287–1292.

Mathias Creutz and Krista Lagus. 2007. Unsupervised models for morpheme segmentation and morphology learning. *ACM Transactions on Speech and Language Processing (TSLP)*, 4(1):3.

Aleksandr Drozd, Anna Gladkova, and Satoshi Matsuoka. 2015. Discovering aspectual classes of russian verbs in untagged large corpora. In *2015 IEEE International Conference on Data Science and Data Intensive Systems*, pages 61–68.

Aleksandr Drozd, Anna Gladkova, and Satoshi Matsuoka. 2016. Word embeddings, analogies, and machine learning: Beyond king - man + woman = queen. In *COLING*.

Manaal Faruqui, Jesse Dodge, Sujay Kumar Jauhar, Chris Dyer, Eduard Hovy, and Noah A Smith. 2015. Retrofitting word vectors to semantic lexicons. In *Proceedings of the 2015 Conference of the North American Chapter of the Association for Computational Linguistics: Human Language Technologies*, pages 1606–1615.

Lev Finkelstein, Evgeniy Gabrilovich, Yossi Matias, Ehud Rivlin, Zach Solan, Gadi Wolfman, and Eytan Ruppin. 2001. Placing search in context: The concept revisited. In *WWW*, pages 406–414. ACM.

Anna Gladkova, Aleksandr Drozd, and Satoshi Matsuoka. 2016. Analogy-based detection of morphological and semantic relations with word embeddings: What works and what doesn't. In *NAACL-HLT*, pages 8–15.

Felix Hill, Roi Reichart, and Anna Korhonen. 2016. Simlex-999: Evaluating semantic models with (genuine) similarity estimation. *Computational Linguistics*.

Sepp Hochreiter and Jürgen Schmidhuber. 1997. Long short-term memory. *Neural computation*, 9(8):1735–1780.

Yoon Kim. 2014. Convolutional neural networks for sentence classification. In *EMNLP*, pages 1746–1751.

Yoon Kim, Yacine Jernite, David A Sontag, and Alexander M. Rush. 2016. Character-aware neural language models.

Diederik P Kingma and Jimmy Ba. 2014. Adam: A method for stochastic optimization. *arXiv preprint arXiv:1412.6980*.

Ryan Kiros, Yukun Zhu, Ruslan Salakhutdinov, Richard S Zemel, Antonio Torralba, Raquel Urtasun, and Sanja Fidler. 2015. Skip-thought vectors. In *NIPS*, pages 3294–3302.

Angeliki Lazaridou, Marco Marelli, Roberto Zamparelli, and Marco Baroni. 2013. Compositional-ly derived representations of morphologically complex words in distributional semantics. In *ACL (1)*, pages 1517–1526.

Yann LeCun. 1998. Gradient-based learning applied to document recognition.

Omer Levy and Yoav Goldberg. 2014a. Dependency-based word embeddings. In *ACL*, pages 302–308.

Omer Levy and Yoav Goldberg. 2014b. Linguistic regularities in sparse and explicit word representations. In *CoNLL*, pages 171–180.

Bofang Li, Tao Liu, Zhe Zhao, Buzhou Tang, Aleksandr Drozd, Anna Rogers, and Xiaoyong Du. 2017. Investigating Different Syntactic Context Types and Context Representations for Learning Word Embeddings. In *EMNLP*, pages 2411–2421.

Wang Ling, Chris Dyer, Alan W. Black, Isabel Trancoso, Ramon Fermandez, Silvio Amir, Luís Marujo, and Tiago Luís. 2015. Finding function in form: Compositional character models for open vocabulary word representation. In *EMNLP*.

Minh-Thang Luong and Christopher D. Manning. 2016. Achieving open vocabulary neural machine translation with hybrid word-character models. *CoRR*, abs/1604.00788.

Thang Luong, Richard Socher, and Christopher D Manning. 2013. Better word representations with recursive neural networks for morphology. In *CoNLL*, pages 104–113.

Andrew L. Maas, Raymond E. Daly, Peter T. Pham, Dan Huang, Andrew Y. Ng, and Christopher Potts. 2011. Learning word vectors for sentiment analysis. In *ACL*, pages 142–150.

Tomas Mikolov, Ilya Sutskever, Kai Chen, Gregory S. Corrado, and Jeffrey Dean. 2013. Distributed representations of words and phrases and their compositionality. In *NIPS*, pages 3111–3119.

Tomáš Mikolov, Ilya Sutskever, Anoop Deoras, Hai-Son Le, Stefan Kombrink, and Jan Cernocky. 2012. Subword language modeling with neural networks. *preprint (http://www. fit. vutbr. cz/imikolov/rnnlm/char. pdf)*.

Andriy Mnih and Geoffrey E. Hinton. 2007. Three new graphical models for statistical language modelling. In *ICML*, pages 641–648.

Tetsuji Nakagawa, Kentaro Inui, and Sadao Kurohashi. 2010. Dependency tree-based sentiment classification using crfs with hidden variables. In *NAACL*, pages 786–794. Association for Computational Linguistics.

Bo Pang and Lillian Lee. 2004. A sentimental education: Sentiment analysis using subjectivity summarization based on minimum cuts. In *ACL*, pages 271–278. Association for Computational Linguistics.

Bo Pang and Lillian Lee. 2005. Seeing stars: Exploiting class relationships for sentiment categorization with respect to rating scales. In *ACL*, pages 115–124. Association for Computational Linguistics.

Yuval Pinter, Robert Guthrie, and Jacob Eisenstein. 2017. Mimicking word embeddings using subword rnns. In *EMNLP*.

Siyu Qiu, Qing Cui, Jiang Bian, Bin Gao, and Tie-Yan Liu. 2014. Co-learning of word representations and morpheme representations. In *COLING*, pages 141–150.

Kira Radinsky, Eugene Agichtein, Evgeniy Gabrilovich, and Shaul Markovitch. 2011. A word at a time: computing word relatedness using temporal semantic analysis. In *WWW*, pages 337–346. ACM.

Anna Rogers, Aleksandr Drozd, and Bofang Li. 2017. The (Too Many) Problems of Analogical Reasoning with Word Vectors. In *Proceedings of the 6th Joint Conference on Lexical and Computational Semantics (* SEM 2017)*, pages 135–148.

Cicero Nogueira dos Santos and Bianca Zadrozny. 2014. Learning character-level representations for part-of-speech tagging. In *ICML*.

Mike Schuster and Kuldip K. Paliwal. 1997. Bidirectional recurrent neural networks. *IEEE Trans. Signal Processing*, 45(11):2673–2681.

Rico Sennrich, Barry Haddow, and Alexandra Birch. 2016. Neural machine translation of rare words with subword units. *CoRR*, abs/1508.07909.

Richard Socher, Alex Perelygin, Jean Y Wu, Jason Chuang, Christopher D Manning, Andrew Y Ng, and Christopher Potts. 2013. Recursive deep models for semantic compositionality over a sentiment treebank. In *EMNLP*, volume 1631, page 1642. Citeseer.

Henning Sperr, Jan Niehues, and Alex Waibel. 2013. Letter n-gram-based input encoding for continuous space language models. In *Proceedings of the Workshop on Continuous Vector Space Models and their Compositionality*, pages 30–39.

Seiya Tokui, Kenta Oono, Shohei Hido, and Justin Clayton. 2015. Chainer: a next-generation open source framework for deep learning. In *Proceedings of workshop on machine learning systems (LearningSys) in the twenty-ninth annual conference on neural information processing systems (NIPS)*, volume 5.

Torsten Zesch, Christof Müller, and Iryna Gurevych. 2008. Using wiktionary for computing semantic relatedness. In *AAAI*, volume 8, pages 861–866.

Xiang Zhang, Junbo Zhao, and Yann LeCun. 2015. Character-level convolutional networks for text classification. In *NIPS*, pages 649–657.

Zhe Zhao, Tao Liu, Shen Li, Bofang Li, and Xiaoyong Du. 2017. Ngram2vec: Learning improved word representations from ngram co-occurrence statistics. In *Proceedings of the 2017 Conference on Empirical Methods in Natural Language Processing*, pages 244–253.

Discovering Phonesthemes with Sparse Regularization

Nelson F. Liu[1,2], Gina-Anne Levow[2], and Noah A. Smith[1]

[1]Paul G. Allen School of Computer Science & Engineering, University of Washington, Seattle, WA, USA
[2]Department of Linguistics, University of Washington, Seattle, WA, USA
{nfliu,nasmith}@cs.washington.edu, levow@uw.edu

Abstract

We introduce a simple method for extracting non-arbitrary form-meaning representations from a collection of semantic vectors. We treat the problem as one of feature selection for a model trained to predict word vectors from subword features. We apply this model to the problem of automatically discovering phonesthemes, which are submorphemic sound clusters that appear in words with similar meaning. Many of our model-predicted phonesthemes overlap with those proposed in the linguistics literature, and we validate our approach with human judgments.

1 Introduction

Linguists have long held that language is arbitrary, or that a word's phonetic and orthographic forms have no relation to its meaning (de Saussure, 1916). For example, there is nothing about an apple that suggests that *apple* is the proper word for it—this link between meaning and the representation in language is arbitrary. Arbitrariness is a defining feature of human language, and it is a key component of the design features of language proposed by Hockett (1960).

Despite this, work over the last decades has revealed several exceptions to the arbitrariness of language. One such exception is iconicity, where the form of a word directly resembles its meaning. For example, Ohala (1984) showed that speakers tend to associate vowels with high acoustic frequency with smaller objects, while vowels with low acoustic frequency are associated with larger objects. In this case, speakers make a link between the phonetic form of a word and its perceived meaning because of an innate belief that smaller entities emit higher-frequency vowels while larger entities tend to emit low-frequency vowels.

Similarly, Köhler (1929) and Ramachandran and Hubbard (2001) observed a non-arbitrary connection between the shapes of objects and speech sounds. American college undergraduates and Tamil speakers were presented with a jagged shape and a rounded shape and asked which is *"kiki"* and which is *"bouba"*. In both groups, 95% to 98% selected the jagged shape as *"kiki"* and the rounded shape as *"bouba"*, demonstrating that the human brain connects sounds to shapes in a consistent way. D'Onofrio (2014) posits that the rounded shape is commonly named *"bouba"* since the mouth forms a rounded shape in producing the word, whereas pronouncing *"kiki"* requires a tighter, more angular mouth shape that seems more apt for the jagged object. In this case, there is a strong, non-arbitrary link between the articulatory properties of the sound and their perceived meaning.

Phonesthemes are another exception to the arbitrariness of language. Phonesthemes are non-compositional, submorphemic phonetic units that consistently occur in words with similar meanings. For example, the word-initial *gl-*, occurs at the beginning of many English words relating to light or vision, like *glint, glitter, gleam, glamour*, etc. (Hutchins, 1998; Bergen, 2004). The work of Hutchins (1998) includes a compilation of 46 phonesthemes proposed by linguists.

There is a body of previous work suggesting that phonesthemes are units in the mental lexicon of native speakers. For example, the work of Hutchins (1998), Magnus (2000), and Bergen (2004) uses priming experiments and other methods from psycholinguistics to demonstrate that phonesthemes significantly affect native speaker reaction times in a range of language processing tasks. In another line of work, Otis and Sagi (2008) and Abramova and Fernández (2016) verify phonesthemes by analyzing whether the words containing a given phonestheme are more semantically similar than expected by chance, where se-

Proceedings of the Second Workshop on Subword/Character LEvel Models, pages 49–54
New Orleans, Louisiana, June 6, 2018. ©2018 Association for Computational Linguistics

mantic similarity is derived from a distributional semantic model.

While there has been much work in verifying previously proposed phonesthemes, there has been little work on automatically discovering new ones. In this work, our goal is to identify the likely phonesthemes of a language from a collection of semantic vectors. We do this by identifying the character or phoneme sequences that are predictive of word meaning by training a model to predict word vectors from subword features. Then, we use standard feature selection techniques to find a subset of features that best predict the vectors; this subset of features contains the model-predicted phonesthemes. Lastly, we validate the model-predicted English phonesthemes with human judgments and also find that many of our predicted phonesthemes overlap with those documented in previous work.

2 Method

To extract phonesthemes from a set of vectors, we want to find submorphemic units (e.g., character or phoneme n-grams) that are highly predictive of word meaning. We approach this problem through the lens of feature subset selection: given a model capable of predicting semantic vectors from submorpheme information, our goal is to select the subset of submorphemes (model features) that are most predictive. Intuitively, if a submorpheme is especially predictive of the word vectors, then it may be a meaning-bearing phonestheme.

We use linear regression to predict word vectors from binary feature vectors that encode the submorphemes occurring in a surface form. We use sparse regularization to select relevant features from this model, which enables it to automatically choose a subset of the submorpheme features that predict the vectors (our predicted phonesthemes).

Specifically, we regularize our linear regression model with the elastic net (Zou and Hastie, 2005). We used `scikit-learn` (Pedregosa et al., 2011) to train our models, and we tune the L_1 and L_2 regularization strengths on held-out error in 5-fold cross-validation.

Mitigating the Effect of Morphemes A principal concern is that the model will detect morphemes rather phonesthemes. Many past studies on the relationship between form and meaning in language (Shillcock et al., 2001; Monaghan et al., 2014; Gutiérrez et al., 2016; Dautriche et al., 2017) mitigated this concern by only considering

monomorphemic words, discarding a large fraction of the lexicon in the process.

We take a different approach to this problem by proposing a two-step model designed to mitigate the effect of morphemes. We begin by training an unregularized linear regression model to predict semantic vectors from morpheme-level features. Then, we use the residuals of this first stage morpheme-level model as the new target vectors for the sparsely regularized phonestheme extraction model. This removes the components of the word vector that are predictable from morpheme-level information, leaving only the aspects of word meaning not covered by morphology.

We use the the morphological analyses in the CELEX lexical database (Baayen et al., 1996) to compile a list of morphemes, which is used to create the morpheme-level feature vectors. We also use this list to remove any morphemes that may appear in the final model output.

3 Data

For our experiments, we use 300-dimensional GloVe (Pennington et al., 2014) English word embeddings trained on the cased Common Crawl. Many of the terms in the set of pretrained vectors are not English words. As a first attempt toward removing non-English words and named entities, we discard types that are not alphabetical or not completely lowercased. In addition, it's unlikely that rare words or very common words will contribute to the formation of sound-meaning associations (Hutchins, 1998). To further filter these rare or common words (and remove additional non-English types), we remove types that either occur less than 1000 times in the Gigaword corpus or in more than half of all Gigaword documents. Lastly, we remove types that share the same lemma if the lemma is also in the set of filtered word vectors. After this process, we are left with 7889 types out of the original 2.2 million.

We phonemicize our vectors by associating each word's vector to the word's ARPAbet symbol sequence, as provided in the CMU Pronouncing Dictionary (Carnegie Mellon University, 2014). If multiple types have the same ARPAbet symbol sequence (and are thus homophones), we discard them all. We also do not use types that are not in the CMU Pronouncing Dictionary. Phonemicizing the filtered set of vectors results in a set of 6633 vectors.

Note that our model can be applied using either orthographic or phonemicized vectors. Phonesthemes are an inherently phonetic phenomenon, which suggests that it is ideal to model the features at the phoneme level. However, using character-level features, in some cases, will be a reasonable approximation, especially since many of our extracted phonesthemes have a consistent orthographic representation. We release code for preprocessing data and training the models at `http://nelsonliu.me/papers/phonesthemes/`.

4 Experiments and Results

The candidate phonesthemes considered by the model are the word-initial phoneme bigram sequences that occur more than five times in our set of phonemicized vectors; we set a frequency threshold for feature inclusion since rare prefixes are unlikely to carry meaning. Each word's feature vector is a one-hot encoding of its bigram phoneme prefix. We choose to focus on word-initial bigrams since the bulk of prior work in linguistics has also focused on phonesthemes in this position. However, our method easily extends to larger subword units (e.g., trigrams), candidate phonesthemes within or at the end of a word, even other languages; we leave analysis of phonesthemes of other sizes, in different positions, and of different languages for future work.

We train our two-stage model on the phonemicized vectors; the features that are assigned a nonzero weight are our model-predicted phonesthemes. The features of our morpheme-level model are binary indicator features corresponding to 181 different morphemes extracted from the CELEX2 database. In total, our phonestheme extraction model considers 307 candidate phonesthemes; tuning the regularization strength on held-out error in 5-fold cross-validation results in a model that selects 123 candidate phonesthemes as predictive. The phoneme bigrams corresponding to the 30 features with the highest absolute model weight are in Table 1. Qualitatively, the words with the lowest error under the model containing each selected phonestheme candidate seem semantically coherent.

Many of the phonesthemes identified by our model have been proposed and validated by past work. 13 of the top 15 model-predicted phonesthemes were in Hutchins' set of 17 proposed word-

ARPAbet Sequence	Character Sequence	Model Example Words
† * S N	sn-	sneaks, snubs, sniffs
* S K	sc-/sk-	screwing, squelched, scurry
* K R	cr-	crunched, cringed, crummy
* S P	sp-	spiffy, splendidly, spunky
B R	br-	brags, brouhaha, brutish
* G R	gr-	griping, grumbles, grandly
* T R	tr-	tryst, trounce, truism
* S T	st-	stupendous, startlingly, stunner
† * B L	bl-	blase, blithely, blankly
* F L	fl-	flaunted, flowered, fluff
† * G L	gl-	glossed, gleam, glamor
* S L	sl-	slouch, slogged, slime
† * D R	dr-	droll, dreamer, drifter
† * S W	sw-	swoon, swoops, swipes
W IH1	wi-	wimpy, willy, wince
K AE1	ca-	candied, caffeinated, cataclysm
P AE1	pa-	pantry, pathogen, pancake
S IH1	sy-/si-	syllable, simulators, synchronize
F R	fr-	froth, frock, freaks
M AE1	ma-	mallet, masts, manor
P EH1	pe-	pendant, pelt, petulant
M EH1	me-	meld, meditate, memorized
M AH1	mu-	mumbled, mummies, mutter
* K L	cl-	clumsily, clunky, claustrophobic
S EH1	se-/ce	sensuous, celibate, celebrants
AH0 B	ob-	obliterate, abridged, obliquely
B AA1	ba-/bo-	barbarous, bogs, barbers
P L	pl-	pled, pliable, platoons
K AO1	co-	corset, coroners, corduroy
F EH1	fe-	fairest, fender, feds

Table 1: The 30 model-predicted phonesthemes with the highest absolute model weight and their typical orthographic representation. The model example words were selected from the 10 phonestheme-bearing words with the lowest model error. * indicates a phonestheme identified by Hutchins (1998). † indicates a phonestheme with statistical support from Otis and Sagi (2008).

initial phoneme bigram phonesthemes. This is an improvement over past work; Otis and Sagi (2008) identified 8 as statistically significant, with a hypothesis space restricted to 50 pre-specified word beginnings and endings. Gutiérrez et al. (2016) also identified 8, but with a much larger hypothesis space of 225 candidates. Our model considers an even larger hypothesis space of 307 candidate phonesthemes, which are all automatically extracted from the set of word vectors.

Validating Phonesthemes with Human Judgments Following the method of Hutchins (1998) and Gutiérrez et al. (2016), we empirically evaluate our phonesthemes by soliciting naïve human judgments about how well-suited a word's form is to its meaning.

We randomly selected 5 words containing each

of the top 15 model-selected phonesthemes and 5 words containing 15 random phonestheme candidates that were not selected by the model, for a total of 150 words.

We recruited native English-speaking participants through Mechanical Turk, and asked them to judge how well each word fits its meaning on a Likert scale from 1 to 5. 150 words is too many judgments for a single HIT (annotators would become fatigued and words might start to lose meaning). As a result, we randomly divided the task into 10 different HITs, each with 15 of the words to be tested. We required Amazon Mechanical Turk Masters status for the crowdworkers and compensated them $0.20 per HIT; each word received 30 ratings.

Following Hutchins (1998), we compute ratings for each candidate phonestheme by averaging the rating of the words that contain it. On average, model-predicted phonesthemes were rated 0.58 points higher than unselected phonestheme candidates (3.66 versus 3.08, respectively). To assess whether this difference is statistically significant, we use the one-tailed Mann-Whitney U test (Mann and Whitney, 1947) since the data is ordinal and unpaired. Based on the results of the test, we reject the null hypothesis that the average rating of words containing model-selected phonesthemes is *not greater* than the average rating of words that contain phonesthemes not selected by the model ($p < 10^{-9}$).

Figure 1 plots the human ratings of the top 15 model-selected phonesthemes against their absolute weight under the model; there is a weak positive correlation ($r = 0.081$).

2 of the 15 model-predicted phonesthemes with the highest absolute weight were not previously proposed by (Hutchins, 1998): *br-* and *wi-*. Both of these sound clusters seem like plausible phonesthemes. To the authors, the *br-* cluster evokes the idea of a raw, almost uncultured force, with words like *"brags," "brutish,"* and *"brusque"* appearing among the words with the lowest error under the model. The types containing the word-initial *wi-* cluster with the lowest error under the model seem to convey fragility: *"wimpy," "wince,"* and *"weak."*

From Figure 1, we can see that the *br-* phonestheme candidate received a very high model weight, but received lower ratings on average from human annotators. On the other hand, the average human rating of the *wi-* phonestheme candi-

date seems in line with its assigned model weight. Future work could further explore whether *br-* and *wi-* have psychological reality to native speakers.

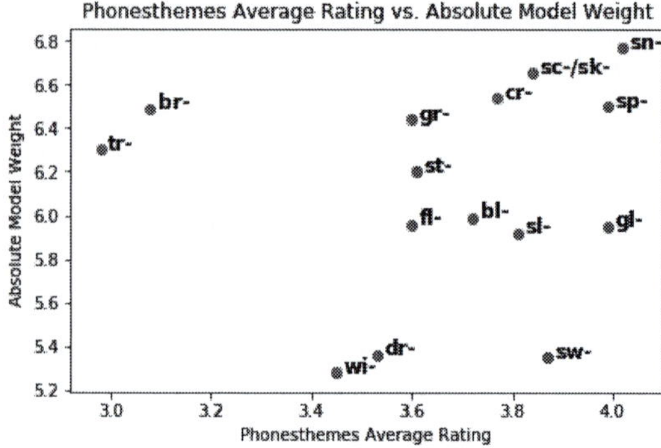

Figure 1: Average human rating versus the absolute model weight for the 15 selected phonesthemes with the highest absolute model weight.

5   Related Work

Several psycholinguistic studies have shown that native speakers associate certain sounds with a particular meaning, and phonesthemes have been identified in languages from English (Wallis, 1699; Firth, 1930) to Swedish (Abelin, 1999) and Japanese (Hamano, 1998). Bergen (2004) additionally demonstrates that phonesthemes affect online implicit language processing, and Parault and Schwanenflugel (2006) suggest that they play a role in language acquisition.

In recent years, the work of Otis and Sagi (2008) and Abramova and Fernández (2016) used computational methods to automatically detect and validate phonesthemes by examining whether words that contain a candidate phonestheme are more semantically similar than predicted by chance, according to a distributional semantic model. Dautriche et al. (2017) analyze lexicons of Dutch, English, German, and French and find that the space of monomorphemic word forms is clumpier than what would be expected by chance, according to lexical, phonological, and network measures.

Most similar to our work is that of Gutiérrez et al. (2016), who introduce an algorithm for learning weighted string edit distances that minimize kernel regression error and use it to detect systematic form-meaning relationships within language. Our model uses linear regression between candidate phonestheme features and semantic vectors. In addition, our model directly selects the predicted phonesthemes with sparse regularization; their model instead provides a systematicity score for each type, and they extract phonesthemes by taking the word-beginnings with mean errors lower than predicted by a random distribution of errors across the lexicon.

6 Conclusion

In this work, we present a simple model for extracting non-systematic form-meaning relationships from a collection of word vectors. Our model is a sparsely regularized linear regression model that seeks to predict a word's semantic vector from a feature vector that encodes information about the candidate phonesthemes it contains; the sparse solutions of the regression problem have the effect of automatically selecting the features that are most predictive of word meaning, which we take as predicted phonesthemes.

We also develop a simple and effective two-stage approach for mitigating the effect of morphemes in the model. We initially train a model to map from morpheme-level features to word vectors, and then use the residuals of the morpheme-level model as the targets for the downstream phonestheme extraction model.

We empirically compare our model's predicted phonesthemes and find that many were previously proposed by linguists. We verified our results with human judgments of proposed and unselected phonesthemes, and annotators believe that words with a model-selected phonestheme "fit their meaning" more than words that contain a candidate phonestheme that was not selected by the model.

Acknowledgments

NL received support from a University of Washington Mary Gates Research Scholarship and a Washington Research Foundation Fellowship. This work was supported in part by NSF grant IIS-1562364. This work was also supported in part by a hardware gift from NVIDIA Corporation.

References

Åsa Abelin. 1999. *Studies in sound symbolism*. Ph.D. thesis, University of Gothenburg.

Ekaterina Abramova and Raquel Fernández. 2016. Questioning arbitrariness in language: A data-driven study of conventional iconicity.

R. Harald Baayen, Richard Piepenbrock, and Léon Gulikers. 1996. CELEX2.

Benjamin K Bergen. 2004. The psychological reality of phonaesthemes. *Language*, 80(2):290–311.

Carnegie Mellon University. 2014. The CMU Pronouncing Dictionary v0.7b. http://www.speech.cs.cmu.edu/cgi-bin/cmudict.

Isabelle Dautriche, Kyle Mahowald, Edward Gibson, Anne Christophe, and Steven T. Piantadosi. 2017. Words cluster phonetically beyond phonotactic regularities. *Cognition*, 163:128–145.

Annette D'Onofrio. 2014. Phonetic detail and dimensionality in sound-shape correspondences: Refining the bouba-kiki paradigm. *Language and Speech*, 57(3):367–393.

John Firth. 1930. *Speech*. Oxford University Press.

E. Dario Gutiérrez, Roger Levy, and Benjamin Bergen. 2016. Finding non-arbitrary form-meaning systematicity using string-metric learning for kernel regression. In *Proc. of ACL*.

Shoko Hamano. 1998. *The Sound-Symbolic System of Japanese*. Cambridge University Press.

Charles F. Hockett. 1960. The Origin of Speech. In *Scientific American*, volume 203, pages 88–96.

Sharon Suzanne Hutchins. 1998. *The psychological reality, variability, and compositionality of English phonesthemes*. Ph.D. thesis, Emory University.

Wolfgang Köhler. 1929. *Gestalt psychology*.

Margaret Magnus. 2000. *What's in a Word? Evidence for Phonosemantics*. Ph.D. thesis, University of Trondheim.

Henry B. Mann and Donald R. Whitney. 1947. On a test of whether one of two random variables is stochastically larger than the other. *The Annals of Mathematical Statistics*, pages 50–60.

Padraic Monaghan, Richard C Shillcock, Morten H Christiansen, and Simon Kirby. 2014. How arbitrary is language? *Philosophical Transactions of the Royal Society of London B: Biological Sciences*, 369(1651).

John J Ohala. 1984. An Ethological Perspective on Common Cross-Language Utilization of F0 of Voice. *Phonetica*, 41(1):1–16.

Katya Otis and Eyal Sagi. 2008. Phonaesthemes: A corpus-based analysis. In *Proc. of CogSci*.

Susan J Parault and Paula J Schwanenflugel. 2006. Sound-symbolism: A piece in the puzzle of word learning. *Journal of psycholinguistic research*, 35(4):329.

F. Pedregosa, G. Varoquaux, A. Gramfort, V. Michel, B. Thirion, O. Grisel, M. Blondel, P. Prettenhofer, R. Weiss, V. Dubourg, J. Vanderplas, A. Passos, D. Cournapeau, M. Brucher, M. Perrot, and E. Duchesnay. 2011. Scikit-learn: Machine Learning in Python. *Journal of Machine Learning Research*, 12:2825–2830.

Jeffrey Pennington, Richard Socher, and Christopher D. Manning. 2014. GloVe: Global Vectors for Word Representation. In *Proc. of EMNLP*.

Vilayanur S Ramachandran and Edward M Hubbard. 2001. Synaesthesia – A Window into Perception, Thought and Language. *Journal of Consciousness Studies*, 8(12):3–34.

Ferdinand de Saussure. 1916. *Course in General Linguistics*.

Richard Shillcock, Simon Kirby, Scott McDonald, and Chris Brew. 2001. Filled pauses and their status in the mental lexicon. In *Proc. of DiSS*.

John Wallis. 1699. *Grammar of the English Language*. Oxford.

Hui Zou and Trevor Hastie. 2005. Regularization and variable selection via the Elastic Net. *Journal of the Royal Statistical Society, Series B*, 67:301–320.

Meaningless yet Meaningful: Morphology Grounded Subword-level NMT

Tamali Banerjee
IIT Bombay
Mumbai, India
`tamali@cse.iitb.ac.in`

Pushpak Bhattacharya
IIT Bombay
Mumbai, India
`pb@cse.iitb.ac.in`

Abstract

We explore the use of two independent subsystems, namely Byte Pair Encoding (BPE) and Morfessor as basic units for subword-level neural machine translation (NMT). We have shown that for linguistically distant language-pairs Morfessor-based segmentation algorithm produces significantly better quality translation than BPE. However, for close language-pairs BPE-based subword-NMT may translate better than Morfessor-based subword-NMT. We have proposed a combined approach of these two segmentation algorithms Morfessor-BPE (M-BPE) which outperforms these two baseline systems in terms of BLEU score. Our results are supported by experiments on three language-pairs: English-Hindi, Bengali-Hindi and English-Bengali.

1 Introduction

Subword-level NMT is an NMT approach that can tackle OOV problem. In order to train an NMT (Cho et al., 2014; Sutskever et al., 2014; Bahdanau et al., 2015) model for a language-pair, the size of vocabularies for source and target languages should be constant. But in reality, the vocabulary of a natural language is open. Some words in test data may be absent in system vocabulary. NMT model cannot interpret the semantics of these OOV words. So, translation quality deteriorates as the number of unseen (rare) words increases (Sutskever et al., 2014).

OOV words are mainly of three types described in Table 1. The first type of OOV words needs transliteration. But for translating the second type of OOV words, we need to look deeper. A word based NMT system treats 'house' and 'houses' as two com-

Type	Example
Named entities	'दिल्ली' *Delhi*
Compound words and inflected words	'moonlight', 'examined'
Rare words in reality	'serendipity'

Table 1: Types of OOV words with example.

pletely different words, which limits the coverage of vocabulary. Morphological analyzers tackle this problem by segmenting 'houses' as 'house' and 's'. This way it can cover many words and their inflections too. The third type of OOV words are dealt by leveraging **lexical similarity** between language-pairs. Lexically similar languages share many words (cognates, loan words) with similar spelling, pronunciation and meaning. Subword-level approaches are effective ways for translation of such shared words.

A character n-gram of a word is called a **subword**. It may or may not be meaningful. On the other hand, a **morpheme** is the smallest grammatical meaningful unit of a language. If we segment 'houses' as 'hou'+'ses', then 'hou' and 'ses' will be meaningless subwords. But if we segment 'houses' as 'house'+'s', then 'house' and 's' will be subwords as well as morphemes.

2 Related work

A word can be segmented as BPE (Sennrich et al., 2016), orthographic syllable (Kunchukuttan and Bhattacharyya, 2016), character (Chung et al., 2016; Costa-jussà and Fonollosa, 2016), Huffman encoding (Chitnis and DeNero, 2015). In our experiment we show that, for translation between linguistically close language-pair BPE subword segmentation is suitable, whereas for transla-

Proceedings of the Second Workshop on Subword/Character LEvel Models, pages 55–60
New Orleans, Louisiana, June 6, 2018. ©2018 Association for Computational Linguistics

tion between linguistically distant language-pair Morfessor-based segmentation is suitable. Our proposed subword segmentation approach utilizes benefit of both BPE and Morfessor (Creutz and Lagus, 2006; Smit et al., 2014; Grönroos et al., 2014) and performs well for both linguistically close and distant language-pairs.

3 BPE algorithm

BPE (Gage, 1994) is originally a data compression technique. The main idea behind BPE is- *"Find the most frequent pair of consecutive two character codes in the text, and then substitute an unused code for the occurrences of the pair."* (Shibata et al., 1999)

3.1 BPE as subword unit

BPE works as subword segmentation method for both NMT (Sennrich et al., 2016) and SMT (Kunchukuttan and Bhattacharyya, 2017). In this method, two vocabularies are used: **training vocabulary** and **symbol vocabulary**. Words in training vocabulary are character-sequences followed by an end-of-word symbol. At first, all characters are added to symbol vocabulary. This step is followed by adding the most frequent symbol bigram to the vocabulary, and all its occurrences are replaced by a new symbol (merged symbol bigram). This step is repeated for a number of times, which is a hyperparameter.

Starting from character level as the number of merge operations is increased, primarily frequent character-sequences and then full words are also added as a single symbol. So, the number of merge operations balances between the NMT model vocabulary size and the length of training sentences. Symbol '@@' is used here to indicate the places of segmentations.

3.2 Hyperparameter selection of BPE

Higher number of merge operations adds almost all words to symbol vocabulary. It will prevent the NMT system to translate on subword level segmentation of words.

Using BPE subword segmentation, the average length of sentences is increased as words are broken into subwords. Larger the sentence size, more difficult it becomes for NMT to learn well from them (Bahdanau et al., 2015). So, proper tuning of this hyperparameter is needed. Higher number of merge operations makes the elements more word-like. Lower number of merge operations makes the elements more character-like, where sometimes character-to-character mappings add transliterated words in the translation output.

3.3 Comparison of BPE segmentation with Morfessor

The goal of morphological analyzers such as Morfessor is to segment a word into its **morphs**, the surface forms of morphemes. Comparison between BPE subword segmentation and Morfessor is described below.

- BPE is a greedy approach. Morfessor takes highest probable segmentation of words and deals with local optima by removing and adding word tokens. So, Morfessor produces more acceptable morphological segmentation than BPE.

- Main advantage of BPE is solving OOV problem in two ways: i) some segmentations are almost morphological segmentation, and ii) some segmentations are nearly character-level segmentations. As a result, OOV words are either transliterated or produce partially correct translations. But in absence of some morphs in the dictionary, Morfessor does not produce character-level segmentations. In such cases, it faces OOV problem.

Our Morfessor-based segmentation algorithm takes all the valid words from the corpora and passes these through morfessor. After getting their morphological segmentation, we replace them in data at their respective places. Like BPE, '@@' is used here to indicate the places of segmentation. That means while decoding from subwords we need to join subwords having '@@' signs with next subword.

4 Our approach

The idea behind our proposed combined approach M-BPE comes from comparing BPE and Morfessor. The hypothesis of this approach is- *"Words should be segmented into real morphs. After that, segmentation of morphs into subwords may be beneficial to handle open vocabulary."* Words can be morphologically segmented by using Morfessor. BPE will be helpful for OOV morphs of type 1 and 3 described in section 1. Work-flow of this approach is described below.

Step 1: Use Morfessor on the set of all words from the dataset.

Step 2: Find and replace all occurrences of these words with their segmented form (symbol '**' is used to keep information of segmenting positions). For example- *'googling'* will be segmented into two morphs *'googl**'* and *'ing'*.

Step 3: Learn and apply BPE on that morph-segmented data. Use symbol '@@' for these segmentations. For example, this may segment the word *'googl**'* as *'go@@'*, *'og@@'* and *'l**'*, if *'googl**'* is rarely occurring word in data. It will not merge already segmented subwords followed by symbol'**', because it'll treat already segmented subwords as different elements.

Step 4: Replace symbol '**' with the symbol '@@'. Finally, the word *'googling'* will become *'go@@ og@@ l@@ ing@@'*.

4.1 Hyperparameter selection of M-BPE

With increasing average number of elements per sentence, performance of an NMT model degrades (Bahdanau et al., 2015). Using the same number of merge operations for both BPE and M-BPE produces a higher number of elements per sentence in case of M-BPE than BPE because the Morfessor part of M-BPE increases the number of elements of a sentence before applying the BPE part on it. In order to get a fair comparison between BPE and M-BPE, we have adjusted their hyperparameter in such a way that average numbers of elements per sentence after segmentation become almost same. So, for maintaining that criterion, here we have kept the number of merge operations of M-BPE higher than that of BPE.

5 Experimental setup

There are three systems of subword segmentation in our experiment, namely- BPE, Mor-

fessor and M-BPE. We have used subword-nmt[1] for BPE segmentation, Flatcat (Grönroos et al., 2014) and NLP Indic Library[2] for producing morphological segmentation of English and Indian words.

5.1 Datasets

We have used data from English-Hindi (En-Hi), English-Bengali (En-Bn) and Bengali-Hindi (Bn-Hi) language-pairs from health and tourism domain multilingual parallel Indian Language Corpora Intitiative (ILCI) corpus (Jha, 2010). We clean and tokenize the training corpus. English data was tokenized using the Stanford tokenizer (Klein and Manning, 2003) and then true-cased using *truecase.perl* provided in MOSES toolkit[3]. For Hindi and Bengali data, we tokenized using NLP Indic Library (Kunchukuttan et al., 2014). Then parallel sentences were divided into three parts for training, testing and tuning/validation. For each language-pair, we have 44,777 sentence-pairs in training data, 1,000 sentence-pairs in tuning data and 2,000 sentence-pairs in test data.

5.2 System details

After tokenization, words of source sentences are broken into subwords using a segmentation algorithm. NMT system receives a sequence subwords of a sentence as input and produces the output of a subword-sequence in target language. Then, subwords are combined to produce words in order to get an actual sentence in target language. We have used NEMATUS (Sennrich et al., 2017) as an attention-based encoder-decoder NMT system in our experiment.

6 Results and discussion

The example given below shows the difference among three segmentations:

Example:

Word level: focusing your mind

BPE level: foc@@ us@@ sing your mind

Morfessor level: focus@@ ing your mind

M-BPE level: foc@@ us@@ ing your mind

---

[1]https://github.com/rsennrich/subword-nmt
[2]anoopkunchukuttan.github.io/indic_nlp_library/
[3]http://www.statmt.org/moses/

Fig 1 shows changes in BLEU scores (Papineni et al., 2002) when we train NMT models using sentences with increasing average number of elements (by tuning hyperparameters). Here, two paths indicate two different approaches of segmentation: i) from word level to BPE level, ii) from word level to M-BPE level via Morfessor level.

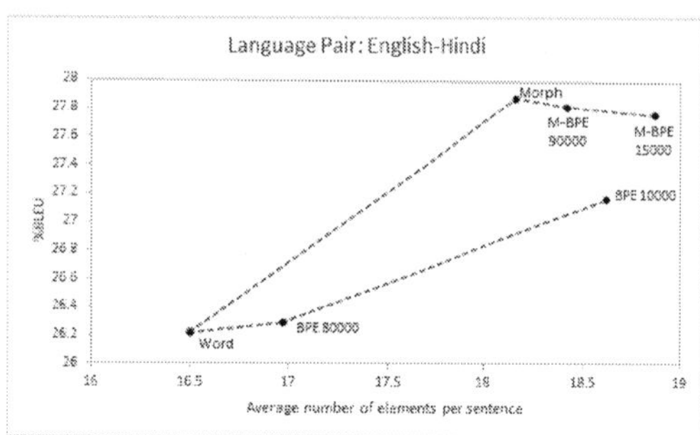

(a) Pair: English-Hindi

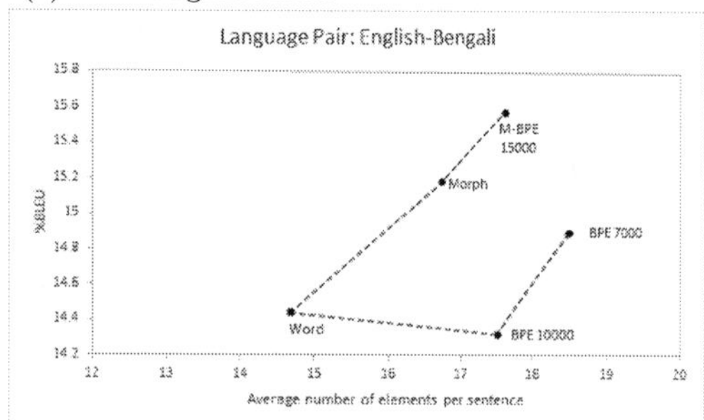

(b) Pair: English-Bengali

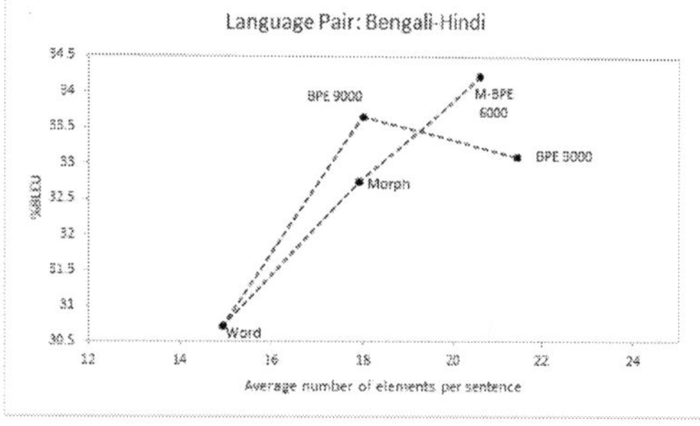

(c) Pair: Bengali-Hindi

Figure 1: Translation accuracies of NMT systems for various translation units (BLEU scores reported).

Table 2 compares among word-level, Morfessor-level, BPE-level and M-BPE level NMT output accuracies for three language-pairs. Tuned numbers of merge operations of BPE and M-BPE, for Bn-Hi, are 3k and 6k. In case of En-Hi, these are 10k and 90k respectively, and for En-Bn these are 7k

and 15k respectively. Translation between lexically close language-pairs like Bn-Hi has more character-to-character mappings than En-Hi. For that reason, Bn-Hi language-pair needs a lower value of hyperparameter than English-Hindi.

Pair	W	M	BPE	M-BPE
Bn-Hi	30.71	32.74	33.09	**34.21**
En-Hi	26.22	**27.87**	27.16	27.81
En-Bn	14.44	15.18	14.89	**15.57**

Table 2: Translation accuracies for various translation units (BLEU scores reported). The reported scores are:- W: word-level, M: Morfessor-level, BPE: BPE-level, M-BPE: M-BPE-level. The values marked in bold indicate the best score for a language pair.

Some findings from the results are listed below.

- For En-Hi and En-Bn language-pairs, Morfessor produces better quality translation than BPE.

- For Bn-Hi language-pair, BPE is capable of producing better translation than Mofessor as segmentation algorithm.

- M-BPE can maintain translation quality for all language-pairs.

In case of Bn-Hi language-pair, BPE helps in improvement of baseline (word-level) translation quality. But in case of En-Hi and En-Bn, it fails to show a considerable amount of improvement. En-Hi and En-Bn language-pairs are quite different from each other in terms of syntactical (word-order, morphology) and lexical similarities. Bengali and Hindi are much closer to each other in comparison with En-Hi and En-Bn. This property of Bn-Hi language-pair helps their translation model to figure out mappings between source and target n-grams. Grammatical rules of languages may not be revealed due to morphologically wrong segmentations. But it hardly affects Bn-Hi translation quality because of their syntactic similarities. Moreover, small subwords add transliterated words in output which is favorable for Bn-Hi translation.

In case of En-Hi and En-Bn, translation models do not easily find mappings between source and target random subwords. It will be useful, only if these subwords are real morphs. For these language-pairs, correct segmentation of word is necessary, not only for getting an accurate translation of word, but also for understanding its grammar (word order and function words). En-Hi and En-Bn language-pairs do not have much lexical similarity; small meaningless subwords do not help in that case; these can even degrade the translation quality.

M-BPE can segment words correctly. It can also produce small subwords by further segmenting morphs. So, by tuning its hyperparameter, we can make it suitable for all language pairs, i.e. linguistically close and linguistically distant language-pairs.

7 Conclusion and future work

As a subword segmentation algorithm, M-BPE outperforms baseline BPE in case of both lexically close and distant language-pairs. However, when compared with baseline Morfessor, improvement due to M-BPE depends on lexical closeness. For lexically close language-pair the improvement is significant. In that case, meaningless BPE subwords play a meaningful role in improving translation quality. Future investigation will be focused on the automatic tuning of hyperparameter for M-BPE.

Acknowledgments

We would like to thank Anoop Kunchukuttan, Kevin Patel and Ajay Anand Verma for their valuable inputs during discussion. We also thank the reviewers for their feedback.

References

Dzmitry Bahdanau, KyungHyun Cho, and Yoshua Bengio. 2015. Neural machine translation by jointly learning to align and translate. In *In Proceedings of the International Conference on Learning Representations (ICLR)*.

Rohan Chitnis and John DeNero. 2015. Variable-length word encodings for neural translation models. In *Proceedings of the 2015 Conference on Empirical Methods in Natural Language Processing*. pages 2088–2093.

Kyunghyun Cho, Bart van Merrienboer, Caglar Gulcehre, Dzmitry Bahdanau, Fethi Bougares, Holger Schwenk, and Yoshua Bengio. 2014. Learning phrase representations using rnn encoder–decoder for statistical machine translation. In *Proceedings of the 2014 Conference on Empirical Methods in Natural Language Processing (EMNLP)*. pages 1724–1734.

Junyoung Chung, Kyunghyun Cho, and Yoshua Bengio. 2016. A character-level decoder without explicit segmentation for neural machine translation. In *Proceedings of the 54th Annual Meeting of the Association for Computational Linguistics (Volume 1: Long Papers)*. volume 1, pages 1693–1703.

Marta R Costa-jussà and José AR Fonollosa. 2016. Character-based neural machine translation. In *Proceedings of the 54th Annual Meeting of the Association for Computational Linguistics (Volume 2: Short Papers)*. volume 2, pages 357–361.

Mathias Creutz and Krista Lagus. 2006. Morfessor in the morpho challenge. In *Proceedings of the PASCAL Challenge Workshop on Unsupervised Segmentation of Words into Morphemes*. Citeseer, pages 12–17.

Philip Gage. 1994. A new algorithm for data compression. *C Users J.* 12(2):23–38. http://dl.acm.org/citation.cfm?id=177910.177914.

Stig-Arne Grönroos, Sami Virpioja, Peter Smit, Mikko Kurimo, et al. 2014. Morfessor flatcat: An hmm-based method for unsupervised and semi-supervised learning of morphology. In *COLING*. pages 1177–1185.

Girish Nath Jha. 2010. The tdil program and the indian langauge corpora intitiative (ilci). In *LREC*.

Dan Klein and Christopher D Manning. 2003. Accurate unlexicalized parsing. In *Proceedings of the 41st Annual Meeting on Association for Computational Linguistics-Volume 1*. Association for Computational Linguistics, pages 423–430.

Anoop Kunchukuttan and Pushpak Bhattacharyya. 2016. Orthographic syllable as basic unit for smt between related languages. In *Proceedings of the 2016 Conference on Empirical Methods in Natural Language Processing*. pages 1912–1917.

Anoop Kunchukuttan and Pushpak Bhattacharyya. 2017. Learning variable length units for smt between related languages via byte pair encoding. In *Proceedings of the First Workshop on Subword and Character Level Models in NLP*. pages 14–24.

Anoop Kunchukuttan, Abhijit Mishra, Rajen Chatterjee, Ritesh Shah, and Pushpak Bhattacharyya. 2014. Sata-anuvadak: Tackling multiway translation of indian languages. *pan* 841(54,570):4–135.

Kishore Papineni, Salim Roukos, Todd Ward, and Wei-Jing Zhu. 2002. Bleu: a method for automatic evaluation of machine translation. In *Proceedings of the 40th annual meeting on association for computational linguistics*. Association for Computational Linguistics, pages 311–318.

Rico Sennrich, Orhan Firat, Kyunghyun Cho, Alexandra Birch, Barry Haddow, Julian Hitschler, Marcin Junczys-Dowmunt, Samuel Läubli, Antonio Valerio Miceli Barone, Jozef Mokry, and Maria Nadejde. 2017. Nematus: a toolkit for neural machine translation. In *Proceedings of the Software Demonstrations of the 15th Conference of the European Chapter of the Association for Computational Linguistics*. Association for Computational Linguistics, Valencia, Spain, pages 65–68. http://aclweb.org/anthology/E17-3017.

Rico Sennrich, Barry Haddow, and Alexandra Birch. 2016. Neural machine translation of rare words with subword units. In *Proceedings of the 54th Annual Meeting of the Association for Computational Linguistics (Volume 1: Long Papers)*. volume 1, pages 1715–1725.

Yusuke Shibata, Takuya Kida, Shuichi Fukamachi, Masayuki Takeda, Ayumi Shinohara, Takeshi Shinohara, and Setsuo Arikawa. 1999. Byte pair encoding: A text compression scheme that accelerates pattern matching.

Peter Smit, Sami Virpioja, Stig-Arne Grönroos, Mikko Kurimo, et al. 2014. Morfessor 2.0: Toolkit for statistical morphological segmentation. In *The 14th Conference of the European Chapter of the Association for Computational Linguistics (EACL), Gothenburg, Sweden, April 26-30, 2014*. Aalto University.

Ilya Sutskever, Oriol Vinyals, and Quoc V Le. 2014. Sequence to sequence learning with neural networks. In *Advances in neural information processing systems*. pages 3104–3112.

Fast Query Expansion for an Accounting Corpus using Sub-word Embeddings

Hrishikesh V. Ganu
Intuit India Development Center
Bangalore, India
hrishikeshvganu@gmail.com

Viswa Datha P.
mail@vishwa.be

Abstract

We present early results from a system under development which uses sub-word embeddings for query expansion in the presence of mis-spelled words and other aberrations. We work for a company which creates accounting software and the end goal is to improve customer experience when they search for help on our "Customer Care" portal. Our customers use colloquial language, non-standard acronyms and sometimes misspell words when they use our Search portal or interact over other channels. However, our Knowledge Base has curated content which leverages technical terms and is in language which is quite formal. This results in the answer not being retrieved even though the answer might actually be present in the documentation (as assessed by a human). We address this problem by creating equivalence classes of words with similar meanings (with the additional property that the mappings to these equivalence classes are robust to mis-spellings) using sub-word embeddings and then use them to fine tune a Search index to improve recall.

1 Introduction

Accounting and taxation is a complex domain-especially for small businesses who might not have the necessary accounting skills but yet need to be compliant with regulations. Hence consumers of accounting software frequently seek advice both about accounting as well as about the product itself.

During an audit process when we started to analyze customers' queries with the help of internal experts, we realised that for a significant number of queries the answers were already available but not retrieved by the search engine because it relies only on keyword based search.

This is primarily due to the following reasons:

1. Self employed and small business owners use colloquial language and terms like *I didn't receive the money customer XYZ owes to me* instead of *I didn't receive my receivables from XYX*

2. Even when customers use accounting terms there are misspellings or structural variants (Form1040 vs Form1040-ES)

1.1 Previous Work

While there have been earlier approaches which deal with these problems through methods like lemmatization, fuzzy matching etc. details of which are given in (Gormley and Tong, 2015), we wanted a method that could be fine-tuned to our dataset without creating hand-crafted rules. Recent progress in creating distributional representations of words has found applications in Information Retrieval (IR) due to work by Zamani and Croft (2017), Korpusik et al. (2017) and Cao and Lu (2017) among others. Some of these models provide the query as an input to a neural network at prediction time while others rely on using the embeddings for query expansion. Our work is in-line with some of these earlier efforts but with a goal of creating an end-end working system that is robust to mis-spellings and other aberrations around the composition of words. Thus in this paper we focus on how we integrated sub-word embeddings with Search systems to create a real-life retrieval system which is currently under development. We demonstrate how this can solve a very practical problem around Information Retrieval from accounting/taxation related corpora.

2 Approach

Our basic approach is to create a search index to enable searching for either the exact word

Proceedings of the Second Workshop on Subword/Character LEvel Models, pages 61–65
New Orleans, Louisiana, June 6, 2018. ©2018 Association for Computational Linguistics

or it's synonyms if they are present in the corpus/vocabulary. In addition our approach is able to map mis-spelled (and hence OOV) words to their "correct" versions on the fly at query time. It involves the following steps:

1. Our expert Customer Care Agents (CCA) create a hand-curated list of "important" words including named entities, actions that customers perform with our products etc.

2. We generate word and sub-word embeddings from our own data and then use these embeddings to create nearest neighbors for the important words. The procedure is similar to that used by Bojanowski et al. (2016) so we don't reproduce it here. Hyperparameter settings that were varied by us are mentioned in Section 3.3.

3. We use the "synonym contraction" mechanism of Elasticsearch to update the index with "synonyms". Since this is a standard procedure we refer the reader to Gormley and Tong (2015) for details. During search, the query is also "analyzed" using the same "analyzer". This can be seen as a kind of query reformulation where $word$ is replaced by $\mathbf{OR}(word, synonym_1, synonym_2...)$. Note that for Out of Vocabulary (OOV) words at query time we get "synonyms" by relying on the embeddings of the sub-words, following the procedure in Bojanowski et al. (2016).

3 Experiments

In this section we discuss the overall objective of the experiment and then mention details about the dataset, pre-processing, training and hyperparameter tuning.

3.1 Objective

As mentioned in Section 2, we wish to understand if an Elasticsearch "Synonyms" file based on sub-word embeddings can lead to a higher recall during search compared to a "Synonyms" file based purely on word embeddings (without sub-word embeddings) especially in the presence of mis-spellings and other perturbations. See Figure 1 for a high level overview of how the "Synonyms" files are created.

Algorithm 1 Offline: Create Nearest Neighbours

Require: Set: RootWords ▷ Hand-crafted set of the core/important words
Require: Hashmap H: RootWord→ ListofWords
Require: Set: V ▷ Vocabulary
Require: Integer K ▷ # neighbours to retrieve
Require:
  function NN(rootWord,V, K)
    return $\{w|w \in K\_NN(rootWord) \cap V\}$
  end function
  function POPULATENN(H,Rootwords,V,K)
    for rootWord $\in$ RootWords **do**
      ▷ Insert word and it's neighbours into H
      H[rootWord]= NN(rootWord, V, K)
      ▷ Remove assigned words from V
      V $\leftarrow$ V \ Set(NN(rootWord,V,K))
    end for
  end function
Ensure: H ▷ Hashmap with root words as keys and K-Nearest Neighbours as values

---

3.2 Dataset and Pre-processing

We realised that the dataset for validating the benefit from this system had to have the following properties:

1. For each query we had to know the matching answer. This was to be used as ground truth.

2. We wanted the answer to be relevant to the matching query but did not want the words in the query to be a subset of words in the answer. This is because had there been good word overlap there wouldn't be a need for query expansion.

After failing to find a well-researched corpus around accounting we decided to use (IRS, 2017), which is a manual written by the Internal Revenue Service (IRS), USA to provide information about personal income tax to taxpayers. While we have also performed experiments on our proprietary knowledge base, for this paper we chose (IRS, 2017) because it is a widely used document and is also available in the public domain. This will enable the larger NLP community to verify and expand upon our findings. Figure 2 shows the layout of a typical page in books like (IRS, 2017). Our basic idea was to use perturbed versions of "headings" (see Section 3.2.1) as queries (perturbed to mimic mis-spellings/typos from real

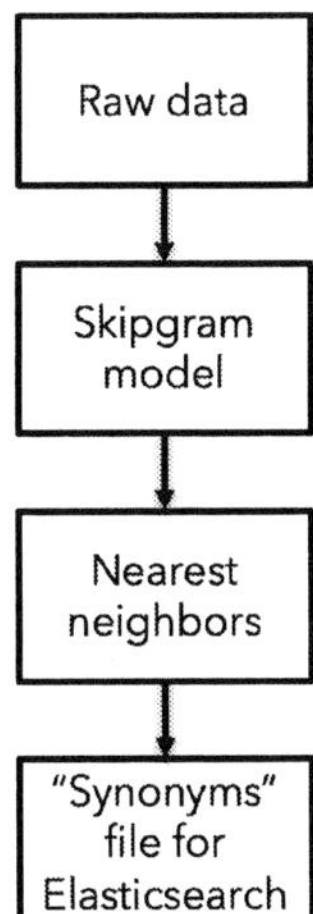

Figure 1: Starting with raw data from (IRS, 2017), a skipgram model (see Section 3.3) was trained, followed by identifying and indexing 10 nearest neighbors per word. This set of nearest neighbors was then provided to Elasticsearch (ES) as a "Synonyms" file which was internally incorporated into the ES index.

users) and to use content in the "body" as documents. Since several downstream models depend on tokenization, we wish to state that for all experiments in this paper we tokenized words using whitespace and using punctuation symbols.

3.2.1 Mis-spelling synthesizer

Our objective here is to compare sub-word embeddings with word embeddings and understand how the robustness to small character level perturbations affects the final recall after search. Since "headings" in books are well formatted and don't have mis-spellings we had to either synthetically generate mis-spelled words or collect statistics around how users mis-spell words in real life. We describe both approaches below.

1. **Synthetic word-level perturbations**: We assume that a word w is a sequence of k characters indexed as c_i so that $w = \{c_1, c_2, .., c_i, .., c_k\}$ and a sentence S is a sequence of n words, indexed as w_j. We select 10% of the queries uniformly at random and create perturbed versions of them. Then for each such query we synthesize perturbed/mis-spelled versions of words by choosing one word uniformly at random (say w_j) to perturb from each sentence and then substitute a random selection of $\lceil 0.20|w_j| \rceil$ adjacent characters by random alphanumeric

characters different from the original.

2. **Mis-spelling statistics learned from user data**: Ideally we wanted to generate perturbed versions of all queries from real-world user data. However because we had limited access to human agents [1], we were able to get only word-level perturbations as against full query level-perturbations from human editors. We followed a process where we first picked the most frequent 200 words out of 903 distinct words forming the vocabulary for queries . Let's call the set of these words as set T. For each such word $w_i \in T$ we asked 5 human annotators to type in these words at a targeted pace of 33 words per minute [2] to simulate the pace at which users type in the real world. This allowed us to collect the set of typed versions S_i of each word w_i (which includes mis-spelled versions as well as the correct word itself) and thus compute a distribution $D_i = Pr(x|\text{correct word is } w_i)$ where $x \in S_i$ for each w_i. Finally, we used these distributions to perturb queries by sampling from D_i for each word in the query that occurred in the top 200. Note that this method does not create true query-level perturbations since whether a word is mis-spelled or not might depend on factors like length of the query, presence of other words etc. Here we look at word mis-spellings when they are typed out in isolation.

3.3 Training skipgram model

A skipgram model was trained on the entire corpus from (IRS, 2017) (using original, unperturbed headings). While in a conventional ML setting this procedure (of using the entire dataset for training without holding out a test sample) might be inappropriate, in our case the main objective is to understand the retrieval systems' robustness to mis-spellings and other character level perturbations. In our setup, such perturbations are not present anywhere in the corpus which is clean and free of all mis-spellings. This means that training the

---

[1] We performed this experiment based on suggestions from reviewers and hence had less than a week to gather and process input from human editors

[2] The average pace for typing is 33 words per minute based on some studies. See `https://en.wikipedia.org/wiki/Typing`

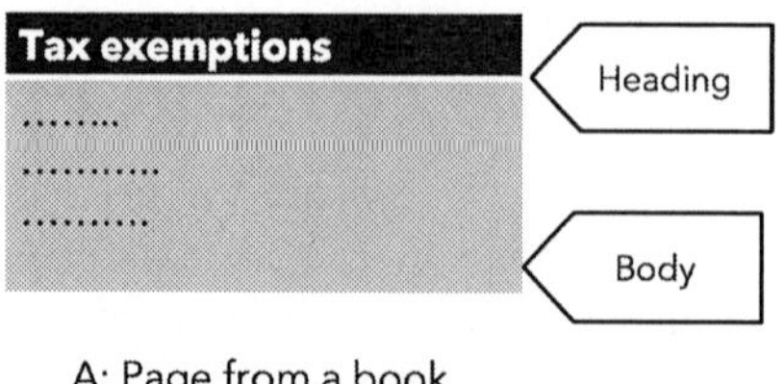

A: Page from a book

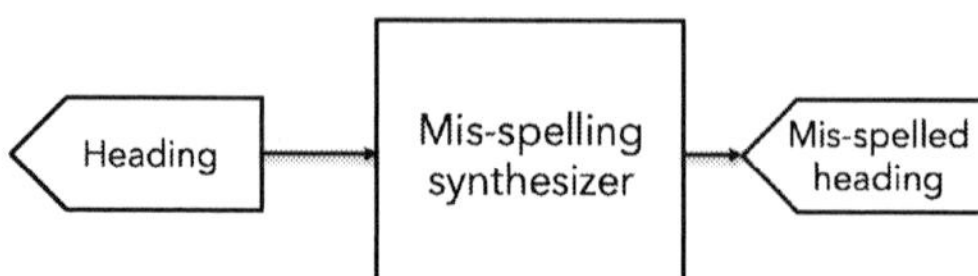

B: Generating mis-spelled headings

Sub-word size	# neigh-bours	Comments
3-6	10	Good quality neighbours. This is the best configuration
2-8	10	Quality worsened
3-6	20	Irrelevant synonyms
2-4	10	Some non-sensical words in synonyms

Table 1: Hyperparameter tuning for generating embeddings

Figure 2: "A: Page from a book" illustrates how a page in a book consists of a heading and some body of text beneath it. This raw corpus was used for training sub-word skipgram models.

"B: Generating mis-spelled headings"" illustrates how we generate misspelled versions of words in "headings" by passing them through a "Mis-spelling synthesizer" (See Section 3.2.1). Mis-spelled headings were used only during search and not for training the skipgram model.

skipgram model on the entire corpus does not prevent us from drawing valid conclusions about the generalization ability of the system as far as robustness to mis-spelled words is concerned. We largely followed the process employed by (Bojanowski et al., 2016) and also leveraged their open-source code [3]. Additionally, because we wanted to retrieve nearest neighbors, we experimented with different settings for the number of neighbors retrieved and sub-word sizes. We relied on internal domain experts to help us determine the configuration with the best synonyms. Details of the experiments and the best configuration chosen are given in Table 1

4 Results

To achieve the objective mentioned in Section 3.1 and in-line with details in Section 3.2, we sent the same set of 805 queries (in our case "headings" perturbed through Section 3.2.1 are queries) to two different Elasticsearch instances: 1) an ES instance having a "Synonyms" file derived from word-level embeddings, called ES_{base} and 2) an instance having a "Synonym" file derived from sub-word embeddings, called $ES_{sub-word}$ (see Figure 3).

4.1 Metrics

We use following notation and metrics:

- $correct_{ES_{base}}$: number of questions for which ES_{base} returned correct results. This is denoted as "# correct baseline" as per the legend in Figure 3

- $correct_{ES_{sub-word}}$: number of questions for which $ES_{sub-word}$ returned correct results. This is denoted as "# correct sub-word" as per the legend in Figure 3

- Recall Ratio (x 100)= $100 \frac{correct_{ES_{sub-word}}}{correct_{ES_{base}}}$

In Figure 3 we report results based on queries generated using the *"Synthetic word-level perturbations"* method in Section 3.2.1. The primary result from this dataset and from some of our experiments on internal proprietary corpora indicate that the Recall Ratio (x 100) metric varies from 110 to 114 depending on how many top results are retrieved and other parameters. This means that we get between a 10% to 14% lift [4] in the number of questions for which correct answers are retrieved when using sub-word embeddings vs when using word embeddings.

Another insight from Figure 3 is that the increase in recall does not come for free. For $K =$

[3] https://github.com/facebookresearch/fastText

[4] Following a suggestion from an anonymous reviewer we also collected statistics on word-level errors by human users and used them to generate perturbed queries (See "Misspellings statistics learned from user data" in Section 3.2.1). The lift was 8% with this more realistic dataset but we could perturb only the top 200 words due to limited availability of editors. Note that this dataset also has some synthetic elements.

10, $\mathbf{ES_{base}}$ gives an empty response 30 times compared with 6 times for $\mathbf{ES_{sub-word}}$. Note that in Figure 3 the total of #correct baseline and #null baseline does not equal total number of queries because for some queries the result set was not empty but contained all "wrong" answers. Similar connotation holds for the corresponding sub-word versions.

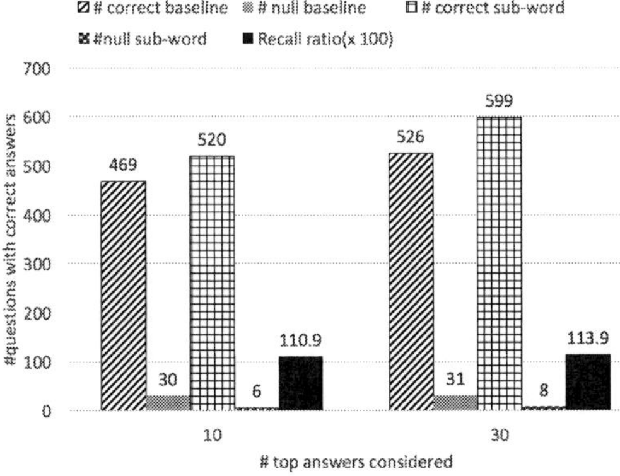

Figure 3: Comparison of the Elasticsearch index using sub-word embeddings, called $\mathbf{ES_{sub-word}}$ with the one using word level embeddings, called $\mathbf{ES_{base}}$. X-axis indicates how many results (say K) from Elasticsearch are considered. E.g: if $K = 10$, we consider only the top 10 results. Y-axis denotes for how many of the 805 queries fired, we received the correct answer in the top K. Because queries are just the perturbed headings, note that for this dataset we assume there's only 1 correct answer per query-the one that appears beneath the heading in (IRS, 2017).

5   Discussion

To test the hypothesis that sub-word embeddings are more robust to spelling error and other perturbations we conducted an experiment with search retrieval as the end goal.

- Through a comparison of sub-word and word level embeddings on a dataset (IRS, 2017) in the public domain, we have demonstrated that using sub-word embeddings for creating the "Synonyms" file for Elasticsearch indeed leads to better recall.

- Since we work in industry we also wish to emphasize that our solution has several features which make it attractive from a practical perspective. In particular, because our solution integrates well with IR systems like ES or Solr, we have very low latency (50ms)

compared to query expansion systems utilizing ML model predictions at query time.

- One of the limitations of this study is that while we have demonstrated a system which increases recall through query expansion, we need to complement it with a layer which can re-rank the retrieved results in a more meaningful way. The default ranking module used by ES does not work well for our use case. Adding such a layer will allow us to measure and track ranking based metrics (like DCG) once the solution goes live and we start receiving user feedback.

Acknowledgments

We thank the two anonymous reviewers for their suggestions to improve the paper in terms of both content and style. Their suggestions, led us to conduct some quick experiments with human editors on how people mis-type words and we have modified the paper to reflect these new results.

References

Piotr Bojanowski, Edouard Grave, Armand Joulin, and Tomas Mikolov. 2016. Enriching word vectors with subword information. *arXiv preprint arXiv:1607.04606*.

Shaosheng Cao and Wei Lu. 2017. Improving word embeddings with convolutional feature learning and subword information. In *AAAI*, pages 3144–3151.

Clinton Gormley and Zachary Tong. 2015. *Elasticsearch: The Definitive Guide*, 1st edition. O'Reilly Media, Inc.

IRS. 2017. *Your Federal Income Tax*. Department of Treasury, Internal Revenue Service, USA.

Mandy Korpusik, Zachary Collins, and James Glass. 2017. Character-based embedding models and reranking strategies for understanding natural language meal descriptions. *Proc. Interspeech 2017*, pages 3320–3324.

Hamed Zamani and W. Bruce Croft. 2017. Relevance-based word embedding. *CoRR*, abs/1705.03556.

A   Supplemental Material

At the following url, we provide examples of the nearest neighbors generated offline for the synonyms file as well as neighbors generated for OOV words at query time. `https://goo.gl/3oQ2xF`

Incorporating Subword Information into Matrix Factorization Word Embeddings

Alexandre Salle   **Aline Villavicencio**
Institute of Informatics
Universidade Federal do Rio Grande do Sul
Porto Alegre, Brazil
alex@alexsalle.com   avillavicencio@inf.ufrgs.br

Abstract

The positive effect of adding subword information to word embeddings has been demonstrated for predictive models. In this paper we investigate whether similar benefits can also be derived from incorporating subwords into counting models. We evaluate the impact of different types of subwords (n-grams and unsupervised morphemes), with results confirming the importance of subword information in learning representations of rare and out-of-vocabulary words.

1 Introduction

Low dimensional word representations (embeddings) have become a key component in modern NLP systems for language modeling, parsing, sentiment classification, and many others. These embeddings are usually derived by employing the distributional hypothesis: that similar words appear in similar contexts (Harris, 1954).

The models that perform the word embedding can be divided into two classes: predictive, which learn a target or context word distribution, and counting, which use a raw, weighted, or factored word-context co-occurrence matrix (Baroni et al., 2014). The most well-known predictive model, which has become eponymous with word embedding, is word2vec (Mikolov et al., 2013a). Popular counting models include PPMI-SVD (Levy et al., 2014), GloVe (Pennington et al., 2014), and LexVec (Salle et al., 2016b).

These models all learn word-level representations, which presents two main problems: 1) Learned information is not explicitly shared among the representations as each word has an independent vector. 2) There is no clear way to represent out-of-vocabulary (OOV) words.

fastText (Bojanowski et al., 2017) addresses these issues in the Skip-gram word2vec model by representing a word by the sum of a unique vector and a set of shared character n-grams (from hereon simply referred to as n-grams) vectors. This addresses both issues above as learned information is shared through the n-gram vectors and from these OOV word representations can be constructed.

In this paper we propose incorporating subword information into counting models using a strategy similar to fastText. We use LexVec as the counting model as it generally outperforms PPMI-SVD and GloVe on intrinsic and extrinsic evaluations (Salle et al., 2016a; Cer et al., 2017; Wohlgenannt et al., 2017; Konkol et al., 2017), but the method proposed here should transfer to GloVe unchanged.

The LexVec objective is modified [1] such that a word's vector is the sum of all its subword vectors. We compare 1) the use of n-gram subwords, like fastText, and 2) unsupervised morphemes identified using Morfessor (Virpioja, 2013) to learn whether more linguistically motivated subwords offer any advantage over simple n-grams.

To evaluate the impact subword information has on in-vocabulary (IV) word representations, we run intrinsic evaluations consisting of word similarity and word analogy tasks. The incorporation of subword information results in similar gains (and losses) to that of fastText over Skip-gram. Whereas incorporating n-gram subwords tends to capture more syntactic information, unsupervised morphemes better preserve semantics while also improving syntactic results. Given that intrinsic performance can correlate poorly with performance on downstream tasks (Tsvetkov et al., 2015), we also conduct evaluation using the VecEval suite of tasks (Nayak et al., 2016), in which all subword models, including fastText, show no significant improvement over word-level models.

We verify the model's ability to represent

---

[1] Our implementation of subword LexVec is available at https://github.com/alexandres/lexvec

66

Proceedings of the Second Workshop on Subword/Character LEvel Models, pages 66–71
New Orleans, Louisiana, June 6, 2018. ©2018 Association for Computational Linguistics

OOV words by quantitatively evaluating nearest-neighbors. Results show that, like fastText, both LexVec n-gram and (to a lesser degree) unsupervised morpheme models give coherent answers.

This paper discusses related word (§2), introduces the subword LexVec model (§3), describes experiments (§4), analyzes results (§5), and concludes with ideas for future works (§6).

2 Related Work

Word embeddings that leverage subword information were first introduced by Schütze (1993) which represented a word of as the sum of four-gram vectors obtained running an SVD of a four-gram to four-gram co-occurrence matrix. Our model differs by learning the subword vectors and resulting representation jointly as weighted factorization of a word-context co-occurrence matrix is performed.

There are many models that use character-level subword information to form word representations (Ling et al., 2015; Cao and Rei, 2016; Kim et al., 2016; Wieting et al., 2016; Verwimp et al., 2017), as well as fastText (the model on which we base our work). Closely related are models that use morphological segmentation in learning word representations (Luong et al., 2013; Botha and Blunsom, 2014; Qiu et al., 2014; Mitchell and Steedman, 2015; Cotterell and Schütze, 2015; Bhatia et al., 2016). Our model also uses n-grams and morphological segmentation, but it performs explicit matrix factorization to learn subword and word representations, unlike these related models which mostly use neural networks.

Finally, Cotterell et al. (2016) and Vúlic et al. (2017) *retrofit* morphological information onto *pre-trained* models. These differ from our work in that we incorporate morphological information at training time, and that only Cotterell et al. (2016) is able to generate embeddings for OOV words.

3 Subword LexVec

The LexVec (Salle et al., 2016a) model factorizes the PPMI-weighted word-context co-occurrence matrix using stochastic gradient descent.

$$PPMI_{wc} = max(0, \log \frac{M_{wc} \, M_{**}}{M_{w*} \, M_{*c}}) \qquad (1)$$

where M is the word-context co-occurrence matrix constructed by sliding a window of fixed size

centered over every *target* word w in the *subsampled* (Mikolov et al., 2013a) training corpus and incrementing cell M_{wc} for every *context* word c appearing within this window (forming a (w, c) pair). LexVec adjusts the PPMI matrix using *context distribution smoothing* (Levy et al., 2014).

With the PPMI matrix calculated, the sliding window process is repeated and the following loss functions are minimized for every observed (w, c) pair and target word w:

$$L_{wc} = \frac{1}{2}(u_w^\top v_c - PPMI_{wc})^2 \qquad (2)$$

$$L_w = \frac{1}{2}\sum_{i=1}^{k} \mathbf{E}_{c_i \sim P_n(c)}(u_w^\top v_{c_i} - PPMI_{wc_i})^2 \qquad (3)$$

where u_w and v_c are d-dimensional word and context vectors. The second loss function describes how, for each target word, k *negative samples* (Mikolov et al., 2013a) are drawn from the smoothed context unigram distribution.

Given a set of subwords S_w for a word w, we follow fastText and replace u_w in eqs. (2) and (3) by u'_w such that:

$$u'_w = \frac{1}{|S_w| + 1}(u_w + \sum_{s \in S_w} q_{hash(s)}) \qquad (4)$$

such that a word is the sum of its word vector and its d-dimensional subword vectors q_x. The number of possible subwords is very large so the function $hash(s)^2$ hashes a subword to the interval $[1, buckets]$. For OOV words,

$$u'_w = \frac{1}{|S_w|} \sum_{s \in S_w} q_{hash(s)} \qquad (5)$$

We compare two types of subwords: simple n-grams (like fastText) and unsupervised morphemes. For example, given the word "cat", we mark beginning and end with angled brackets and use all n-grams of length 3 to 6 as subwords, yielding $S_{cat} = \{\langle ca, at \rangle, cat\}$. Morfessor (Virpioja, 2013) is used to probabilistically segment words into morphemes. The Morfessor model is trained using raw text so it is entirely unsupervised. For the word "subsequent", we get $S_{subsequent} = \{\langle sub, sequent \rangle\}$.

---

[2]http://www.isthe.com/chongo/tech/comp/fnv/

4 Materials

Our experiments aim to measure if the incorporation of subword information into LexVec results in similar improvements as observed in moving from Skip-gram to fastText, and whether unsupervised morphemes offer any advantage over n-grams. For IV words, we perform intrinsic evaluation via word similarity and word analogy tasks, as well as downstream tasks. OOV word representation is tested through qualitative nearest-neighbor analysis.

All models are trained using a 2015 dump of Wikipedia, lowercased and using only alphanumeric characters. Vocabulary is limited to words that appear at least 100 times for a total of 303517 words. Morfessor is trained on this vocabulary list.

We train the standard LexVec (LV), LexVec using n-grams (LV-N), and LexVec using unsupervised morphemes (LV-M) using the same hyper-parameters as Salle et al. (2016a) (window = 2, initial learning rate = .025, subsampling = 10^{-5}, negative samples = 5, context distribution smoothing = .75, positional contexts = True).

Both Skip-gram (SG) and fastText (FT) are trained using the reference implementation[3] of fastText with the hyper-parameters given by Bojanowski et al. (2017) (window = 5, initial learning rate = .025, subsampling = 10^{-4}, negative samples = 5).

All five models are run for 5 iterations over the training corpus and generate 300 dimensional word representations. LV-N, LV-M, and FT use 2000000 buckets when hashing subwords.

For word similarity evaluations, we use the WordSim-353 Similarity (WS-Sim) and Relatedness (WS-Rel) (Finkelstein et al., 2001) and SimLex-999 (SimLex) (Hill et al., 2015) datasets, and the Rare Word (RW) (Luong et al., 2013) dataset to verify if subword information improves rare word representation. Relationships are measured using the Google semantic (GSem) and syntactic (GSyn) analogies (Mikolov et al., 2013a) and the Microsoft syntactic analogies (MSR) dataset (Mikolov et al., 2013b).

We also evaluate all five models on downstream tasks from the VecEval suite (Nayak et al., 2016)[4], using only the tasks for which training and evaluation data is freely available: chunking, sentiment

[3]https://github.com/facebookresearch/fastText
[4]https://github.com/NehaNayak/veceval

Evaluation	LV	LV-N	LV-M	SG	FT
WS-Sim	.749	.748	.746	**.783**	.778
WS-Rel	.627	.627	.625	**.683**	.672
SimLex	.359	**.374**	.366	.371	.367
RW	.461	**.522**	.479	.481	.500
GSem	**80.7**	73.8	**80.7**	78.9	77.0
GSyn	62.8	68.6	63.8	68.2	**71.1**
MSR	49.6	55.0	53.8	57.8	**59.6**
Chunk	90.4	**90.6**	90.5	90.4	90.4
Sentiment	77.0	77.0	77.6	75.3	*77.9*
Questions	*87.4*	*87.4*	87.3	86.6	85.1
NLI	43.3	43.4	43.3	43.4	*43.8*

Table 1: Word similarity (*Spearman's rho*), analogy (% accuracy), and downstream task (% accuracy) results. In downstream tasks, for the same model accuracy varies over different runs, so we report the mean over 20 runs, in which the only significantly ($p < .05$ under a random permutation test) different result is in chunking.

and question classification, and natural language identification (NLI). The default settings from the suite are used, but we run only the *fixed* settings, where the embeddings themselves are not tunable parameters of the models, forcing the system to use only the information already in the embeddings.

Finally, we use LV-N, LV-M, and FT to generate OOV word representations for the following words: 1) "hellooo": a greeting commonly used in instant messaging which emphasizes a syllable. 2) "marvelicious": a made-up word obtained by merging "marvelous" and "delicious". 3) "louisana": a misspelling of the proper name "Louisiana". 4) "rereread": recursive use of prefix "re". 5) "tuzread": made-up prefix "tuz".

5 Results

Results for IV evaluation are shown in table 1, and for OOV in table 2. Like in FT, the use of subword information in both LV-N and LV-M results in 1) better representation of rare words, as evidenced by the increase in RW correlation, and 2) significant improvement on the GSyn and MSR tasks, in evidence of subwords encoding information about a word's syntactic function (the suffix "ly", for example, suggests an adverb). There seems to a trade-off between capturing semantics and syntax as in both LV-N and FT there is an accompanying decrease on the GSem tasks in exchange for gains on the GSyn and MSR tasks. Morphological

Word	Model	5 Nearest Neighbors
"hellooo"	LV-N	hellogoodbye, hello, helloworld, helloween, helluva
	LV-M	kitsos, finos, neros, nonono, theodoroi
	FT	hello, helloworld, hellogoodbye, helloween, joegazz
"marvelicious"	LV-N	delicious, marveled, marveling, licious, marvellous
	LV-M	marveling, marvelously, marveled, marvelled, loquacious
	FT	delicious, deliciously, marveling, licious, marvelman
"louisana"	LV-N	luisana, pisana, belisana, chiisana, rosana
	LV-M	louisy, louises, louison, louiseville, louisiade
	FT	luisana, louisa, belisana, anabella, rosana
"rereread"	LV-N	reread, rereading, read, writeread, rerecord
	LV-M	alread, carreer, whiteread, unremarked, oread
	FT	reread, rereading, read, reiterate, writeread
"tuzread"	LV-N	tuzi, tuz, tuzla, prizren, momchilgrad, studenica
	LV-M	tuzluca, paczk, goldsztajn, belzberg, yizkor
	FT	pazaryeri, tufanbeyli, yenipazar, leskovac, berovo

Table 2: We generate vectors for OOV using subword information and search for the nearest (cosine distance) words in the embedding space. The LV-M segmentation for each word is: $\{\langle \text{hell, o, o, o}\rangle\}$, $\{\langle \text{marvel, i, cious}\rangle\}$, $\{\langle \text{louis, ana}\rangle\}$, $\{\langle \text{re, re, read}\rangle\}$, $\{\langle \text{tu, z, read}\rangle\}$. We omit the LV-N and FT n-grams as they are trivial and too numerous to list.

segmentation in LV-M appears to favor syntax less strongly than do simple n-grams.

On the downstream tasks, we only observe statistically significant ($p < .05$ under a random permutation test) improvement on the chunking task, and it is a very small gain. We attribute this to both regular and subword models having very similar quality on frequent IV word representation. Statistically, these are the words are that are most likely to appear in the downstream task instances, and so the superior representation of rare words has, due to their nature, little impact on overall accuracy. Because in all tasks OOV words are mapped to the "$\langle \text{unk}\rangle$" token, the subword models are not being used to the fullest, and in future work we will investigate whether generating representations for all words improves task performance.

In OOV representation (table 2), LV-N and FT work almost identically, as is to be expected. Both find highly coherent neighbors for the words "hellooo", "marvelicious", and "rereread". Interestingly, the misspelling of "louisana" leads to coherent name-like neighbors, although none is the expected correct spelling "louisiana". All models stumble on the made-up prefix "tuz". A possible fix would be to down-weigh very rare subwords in the vector summation. LV-M is less robust than LV-N and FT on this task as it is highly sensitive to incorrect segmentation, exemplified in the "hellooo" example.

Finally, we see that nearest-neighbors are a mixture of similarly pre/suffixed words. If these pre/suffixes are semantic, the neighbors are semantically related, else if syntactic they have similar syntactic function. This suggests that it should be possible to get *tunable* representations which are more driven by semantics or syntax by a *weighted* summation of subword vectors, given we can identify whether a pre/suffix is semantic or syntactic in nature and weigh them accordingly. This might be possible without supervision using corpus statistics as syntactic subwords are likely to be more frequent, and so could be down-weighted for more semantic representations. This is something we will pursue in future work.

6 Conclusion and Future Work

In this paper, we incorporated subword information (simple n-grams and unsupervised morphemes) into the LexVec word embedding model and evaluated its impact on the resulting IV and OOV word vectors. Like fastText, subword LexVec learns better representations for rare words than its word-level counterpart. All models generated coherent representations for OOV words, with simple n-grams demonstrating more robustness than unsupervised morphemes. In future work, we will verify whether using OOV representations in downstream tasks improves performance. We will also explore the trade-off between semantics and syntax when subword information is used.

References

Marco Baroni, Georgiana Dinu, and Germán Kruszewski. 2014. Dont count, predict! a systematic comparison of context-counting vs. context-predicting semantic vectors. In *Proceedings of the 52nd Annual Meeting of the Association for Computational Linguistics*, volume 1, pages 238–247.

Parminder Bhatia, Robert Guthrie, and Jacob Eisenstein. 2016. Morphological priors for probabilistic neural word embeddings. In *EMNLP*.

Piotr Bojanowski, Edouard Grave, Armand Joulin, and Tomas Mikolov. 2017. Enriching word vectors with subword information. *TACL*, 5:135–146.

Jan A. Botha and Phil Blunsom. 2014. Compositional morphology for word representations and language modelling. In *ICML*.

Kris Cao and Marek Rei. 2016. A joint model for word embedding and word morphology. In *Rep4NLP@ACL*.

Daniel Cer, Mona Diab, Eneko Agirre, Inigo Lopez-Gazpio, and Lucia Specia. 2017. Semeval-2017 task 1: Semantic textual similarity multilingual and crosslingual focused evaluation. In *Proceedings of the 11th International Workshop on Semantic Evaluation (SemEval-2017)*, pages 1–14.

Ryan Cotterell and Hinrich Schütze. 2015. Morphological word-embeddings. In *HLT-NAACL*.

Ryan Cotterell, Hinrich Schütze, and Jason Eisner. 2016. Morphological smoothing and extrapolation of word embeddings. In *ACL*.

Lev Finkelstein, Evgeniy Gabrilovich, Yossi Matias, Ehud Rivlin, Zach Solan, Gadi Wolfman, and Eytan Ruppin. 2001. Placing search in context: The concept revisited. In *Proceedings of the 10th international conference on World Wide Web*, pages 406–414. ACM.

Zellig S Harris. 1954. Distributional structure. *Word*.

Felix Hill, Roi Reichart, and Anna Korhonen. 2015. Simlex-999: Evaluating semantic models with (genuine) similarity estimation. *Computational Linguistics*, 41(4):665–695.

Yoon Kim, Yacine Jernite, David Sontag, and Alexander M. Rush. 2016. Character-aware neural language models. In *AAAI*.

Michal Konkol, Tomas Brychcin, Michal Nykl, and Tomáš Hercig. 2017. Geographical evaluation of word embeddings. In *IJCNLP*.

Omer Levy, Yoav Goldberg, and Israel Ramat-Gan. 2014. Linguistic regularities in sparse and explicit word representations. *CoNLL 2014*, page 171.

Wang Ling, Chris Dyer, Alan W. Black, Isabel Trancoso, Ramon Fermandez, Silvio Amir, Luís Marujo, and Tiago Luís. 2015. Finding function in form: Compositional character models for open vocabulary word representation. In *EMNLP*.

Minh-Thang Luong, Richard Socher, and Christopher D Manning. 2013. Better word representations with recursive neural networks for morphology. *CoNLL-2013*, 104.

Tomas Mikolov, Kai Chen, Greg Corrado, and Jeffrey Dean. 2013a. Efficient estimation of word representations in vector space. *arXiv preprint arXiv:1301.3781*.

Tomas Mikolov, Wen-tau Yih, and Geoffrey Zweig. 2013b. Linguistic regularities in continuous space word representations. In *HLT-NAACL*, pages 746–751.

Jeff Mitchell and Mark Steedman. 2015. Orthogonality of syntax and semantics within distributional spaces. In *Proceedings of the 53rd Annual Meeting of the Association for Computational Linguistics and the 7th International Joint Conference on Natural Language Processing (Volume 1: Long Papers)*, volume 1, pages 1301–1310.

Neha Nayak, Gabor Angeli, and Christopher D. Manning. 2016. Evaluating word embeddings using a representative suite of practical tasks. In *Proceedings of the 1st Workshop on Evaluating Vector-Space Representations for NLP, RepEval@ACL 2016, Berlin, Germany, August 2016*, pages 19–23. Association for Computational Linguistics.

Jeffrey Pennington, Richard Socher, and Christopher D Manning. 2014. Glove: Global vectors for word representation. *Proceedings of the Empiricial Methods in Natural Language Processing (EMNLP 2014)*, 12.

Siyu Qiu, Qing Cui, Jiang Bian, Bin Gao, and Tie-Yan Liu. 2014. Co-learning of word representations and morpheme representations. In *Proceedings of COLING 2014, the 25th International Conference on Computational Linguistics: Technical Papers*, pages 141–150.

Alexandre Salle, Marco Idiart, and Aline Villavicencio. 2016a. Enhancing the lexvec distributed word representation model using positional contexts and external memory. *CoRR*, abs/1606.01283.

Alexandre Salle, Aline Villavicencio, and Marco Idiart. 2016b. Matrix factorization using window sampling and negative sampling for improved word representations. In *Proceedings of the 54th Annual Meeting of the Association for Computational Linguistics, ACL 2016, August 7-12, 2016, Berlin, Germany, Volume 2: Short Papers*. The Association for Computer Linguistics.

Hinrich Schütze. 1993. Word space. In *Advances in neural information processing systems*, pages 895–902.

Yulia Tsvetkov, Manaal Faruqui, Wang Ling, Guillaume Lample, and Chris Dyer. 2015. Evaluation of word vector representations by subspace alignment. In *EMNLP*.

Lyan Verwimp, Joris Pelemans, Hugo Van hamme, and Patrick Wambacq. 2017. Character-word lstm language models. In *EACL*.

Peter; Grnroos Stig-Arne; Kurimo Mikko Virpioja, Sami; Smit. 2013. Morfessor 2.0: Python implementation and extensions for morfessor baseline. D4 julkaistu kehittmis- tai tutkimusraportti tai -selvitys.

Ivan Vúlic, Nikola Mrksic, Roi Reichart, Diarmuid Ó Séaghdha, Steve J. Young, and Anna Korhonen. 2017. Morph-fitting: Fine-tuning word vector spaces with simple language-specific rules. In *Proceedings of the 55th Annual Meeting of the Association for Computational Linguistics, ACL 2017, Vancouver, Canada, July 30 - August 4, Volume 1: Long Papers*, pages 56–68. Association for Computational Linguistics.

John Wieting, Mohit Bansal, Kevin Gimpel, and Karen Livescu. 2016. Charagram: Embedding words and sentences via character n-grams. In *EMNLP*.

Gerhard Wohlgenannt, Nikolay Klimov, Dmitry Mouromtsev, Daniil Razdyakonov, Dmitry Pavlov, and Yury Emelyanov. 2017. Using word embeddings for visual data exploration with ontodia and wikidata. In *BLINK/NLIWoD3@ISWC*.

A Multi-Context Character Prediction Model
for a Brain-Computer Interface

Shiran Dudy and **Steven Bedrick**
Center for Spoken
Language Understanding
Oregon Health & Science University
Portland, OR, USA
{dudy,bedricks}@ohsu.edu

Shaobin Xu and **David A. Smith**
College of Computer
and Information Sciences
Northeastern University
Boston, MA, USA
{shaobinx,dasmith}@ccs.neu.edu

Abstract

Brain-computer interfaces and other augmentative and alternative communication devices introduce language-modeing challenges distinct from other character-entry methods. In particular, the acquired signal of the EEG (electroencephalogram) signal is noisier, which, in turn, makes the user intent harder to decipher. In order to adapt to this condition, we propose to maintain ambiguous history for every time step, and to employ, apart from the character language model, word information to produce a more robust prediction system. We present preliminary results that compare this proposed Online-Context Language Model (OCLM) to current algorithms that are used in this type of setting. Evaluations on both perplexity and predictive accuracy demonstrate promising results when dealing with ambiguous histories in order to provide to the front end a distribution of the next character the user might type.

1 Introduction

Augmentative and alternative communication (AAC) devices are aimed at individuals facing communication disabilities, and aim to enable them to interact with their environment, assisting with both comprehension as well as expression of the individual (Beukelman and Mirenda, 2005; American Speech Language Hearing Association et al., 2004). In particular, a Brain-Computer Interface (BCI) has been employed as an aiding device for patients who have experienced loss of motor control, and who might struggle with producing spoken or written language (Birbaumer et al., 1999; Sellers et al., 2010) (as in e.g. Amyotrophic Lateral Sclerosis). A BCI system measures a user's brain's electrical activity, typically using electroencephalography (EEG), and attempts to infer intent, often in response to stimuli such as row-column scanning.

Communication rates in BCI systems tend to be quite slow. To reduce the prediction time of the next letter in the sequence, one approach is to incorporate language models into AAC devices (Vertanen and Kristensson, 2011), and BCI in particular (Mora-Cortes et al., 2014). The potential advantage of combining a language model with EEG information in a BCI system is twofold: achieving higher accuracy of target predictions, as well as gains in the speed of the process of typing the user's intended string (Speier et al., 2011; Orhan et al., 2011). It may also help with reducing the number of necessary stimuli required for symbol selection (Speier et al., 2016).

Mora-Cortes et al. (2014) describe different types of EEG responses common when employing a typing-based BCI, and in the review of Speier et al. (2016), event-related potentials (ERP) seem to be the prevailing choice in particular. In the RSVP-Keyboard (Orhan et al., 2012), an ERP signal is elicited in response to a rapid display of letters. Other systems such as the P300 (Farwell and Donchin, 1988) present a user with a grid of letters and the ERP signal is retrieved in response to a flash of each row or column.

In such systems, a language model provides the prior distribution that serves as a bias to the EEG evidence when computing the posterior distribution of a symbol as shown in Equation 1

$$p(sym|EEG) = \frac{p(sym)p(EEG|sym)}{p(EEG)} \quad (1)$$

Traditionally, such BCI systems commit to a single decision (given their posterior results), which introduces a problem once the decision is not aligned with the user. One option is to allow for a backspace character, though this poses complex modeling challenges (Fowler et al., 2013). In our system we propose to partly commit to a decision with regard to the user intent, and maintain more than one candidate for every letter selection.

Proceedings of the Second Workshop on Subword/Character LEvel Models, pages 72–77
New Orleans, Louisiana, June 6, 2018. ©2018 Association for Computational Linguistics

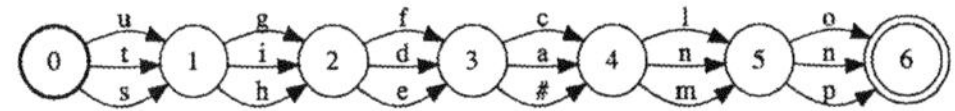

Figure 1: EEG evidence for 6 letter selections

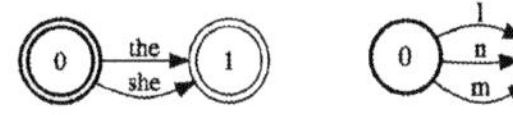

Figure 2: left to right *word history* and *trailing prefix*

This way, the best path is frequently re-evaluated and as a result can revise previously typed strings. Maintaining more than one candidate may reduce frustration among users, and minimize time spent correcting errors. We also, as recommended by Mora-Cortes et al. (2014) and Speier et al. (2016), explicitly incorporate word-level information and mix word-level and character-level language models to improve letter level prediction. Notably, this approach allows our system to support out-of-vocabulary (OOV) words.

Ambiguous input is widely used in traditional Automatic Speech Recognition (Jelinek, 1997) systems along with the Viterbi algorithm (Viterbi, 1967) to find the best path of the utterance bottom-up, from acoustic phoneme units (often triphones) to characters and words (often represented as the $C \circ L \circ G$ composition), and recently in keyboard settings as well by swiping (Ouyang et al., 2017). To the best of our knowledge, it has rarely been explored in the area of BCI, with a notable exception being the work of Speier et al. (2015), who later found it to be intractable due to complexity issues (Speier et al., 2016).

In this work, we present the *Online-Context Language Model* (OCLM) and describe the process of producing prior distributions given EEG evidence as part of our BCI system. Our contributions are specifically in the context of BCI as we integrate word language models (within the system), allow for OOV words to be typed, and optimize over word-level paths to compute optimal priors. Our mixed-context approach achieves superior performance in the face of noisy input compared with a purely character-level model.

2 Methodology

2.1 Overview

To illustrate our method, the steps presented are applied on the input in Figure 1, which depicts a temporal sequence of EEG evidence. Each numbered state represents a selection epoch in which a user has attempted to "type" a letter. Arcs transitioning between nodes i to $i + 1$ represent possible selections, and (though not drawn as such in this figure) are weighted with the normalized EEG likelihoods of time step i retrieved from the BCI.

In this example, the OCLM is currently aiming to provide a prior distribution for the 7th letter selection given the EEG evidence. Assume that the intended string the user wishes to type is "the mo".

The first step taken is to split the EEG history lattice shown in Figure 1 into two parts: one, containing all strings before the last space ("#" in Figure 1), which we will call the "word history" lattice, and another, containing all possible strings *after* the last space, called the *"trailing prefix"* (F_{tp}) as shown in Figure 2.[1]

The *word history* (F_{wh}) represents all possible complete words that the user is assumed to have finished typing. The second part represents the word that the user is assumed to be in the middle of typing, and can be thought of as the set of possible prefixes for the current intended word. We can use this to generate possible word *completions*.

A current in-progress word lattice (F_{cw}) is generated by finding all possible in-vocabulary words that start with the "trailing prefix." By concatenating both the word history lattice (F_{wh}) as well as a lattice of possible in-progress words, and then composing the result with a word-level language model (F_{wLM}), we are able to produce a weighted n-best list of hypothesized words that the user may be trying to produce (F_{top_n}, Equation 2).

$$F_{top_n} = (F_{wh} \| F_{cw}) \circ F_{wLM} \tag{2}$$

$$F_{top_n}^{char} = proj_{char}(F_{top_n} \circ F_{spellout}) \tag{3}$$

$$F_{sym} = F_{top_n}^{char} \cup F_{charLM} \tag{4}$$

$$F_{OCLM} = (F_{tp} \| \sigma) \circ F_{sym} \tag{5}$$

We next take the lattice of "current words", compose that with a word-to-character spellout machine ($F_{spellout}$), project the result into character space (Equation 3), and then take the union of the result with a character language model to produce a "symbol language model" lattice (F_{sym} in Equation 4).

We are now ready to compute probabilities for the likely next symbol the user intends to select. We do this by taking our original trailing prefix

---

[1] The *trailing prefix* shown in figure 2 is simplified for illustrative purposes; in this example, it also includes other paths from state 0 that do *not* include "#". Note also that all paths contain the same number of characters since backspaces are omitted.

lattice (F_{tp}, containing distributions over characters actually selected by the user), concatenating it a character "wild card" machine (σ, representing the next character that the user intends to select to continue F_{tp}), and intersecting the resulting machine with F_{sym} (Equation 5). At this point, we are able to extract a probability distribution over possible character selections by performing weight pushing to the end of the machine, and then examining the final set of arcs in F_{OCLM}. All of these FST operations are implemented with the OpenFst (Allauzen et al., 2007) and OpenGRM-NGRAM (Roark et al., 2012) libraries.

2.2 Out of Vocabulary Words

It is crucial that our system allows its users to enter novel, out-of-vocabulary words, which we support in the following way. Above, we described how we take the lattice of characters making up the current, in-progress word and combine it with a lexicon transducer to produce a weighted lattice of possible word completions. Our approach deals differently and distinguishes between rarely seen words in the training set and completely unseen words. Infrequent words that were seen less than five times but at least once during training are mapped to $<unk>$ word-symbol. In these cases, an attempt to complete a prefix for such a word results in an $<unk>$ word token as a possibility in F_{cw}'s list. F_{wLM} is also trained on these $<unk>$ representations suggesting that $<unk>$ is treated similarly to any other word appearing in the training after the infrequent word was mapped to it (following the process in Equations 2 to 5). However, while the described process applies to uncommon but observed words, when a prefix is part of an *unseen* word and there is no possible completion provided by the lexicon then, $F_{cw} = \emptyset$ and the process is reduced to Equations 4 and 5 such that $F_{sym} = F_{charLM}$. The F_{charLM} contains a failure (ϕ) transition such that for every possible prefix in F_{tp} that is not found in F_{sym} (which in this situation is equivalent to F_{charLM}), we back off to a partial prefix route.

2.3 Word Completion

As described above, while computing the prior distribution over the next character, every new piece of evidence that is added to the system (i.e., each new attempt at character selection by the user) is appended to a "trailing prefix," F_{tp}, which we use to compute hypotheses about the current

words the user might be in the middle of typing. In Equation 2 above, F_{cw} contains all possible in-vocabulary words that the user may be trying to produce, and F_{top_n} is a refined list of those words. This means that our architecture is able to produce both word- and character-level predictions simultaneously, and can easily vary the number of such predictions.

2.4 Auto-correction

While character deletion or insertion events are not auto-corrected in our approach, we address auto-correction to some degree. As described in the main process of computing the prior distribution, there is a frequent re-assessment the previously typed words. This history is recalculated as more EEG evidence of letter selections is introduced; this recalculation occurs mainly when the space character is introduced as it affects the word-boundaries and thus the history. As a result, at each time step, the updated history is re-scored by the word language-model (F_{wLM}), as our estimated most-likely word history may have changed. In Figure 1, for instance, we start with "she" and "the" as possible histories. As character selection continues, we might have "monkey" as a strongly-predicted possible word completion; in this case, F_{wLM} will prioritize "the" over "she," as "the monkey" is more probable than "she monkey". However, if "modifies" were to be judged more likely by F_{top_n}, "she" would get prioritized over "the". Making additional and extended use of this information is part of our future work plan.

3 Experimental Evaluation

In order to evaluate the OCLM, we constructed a simulated character selection task to compare the performance of three different algorithms. The first is a smoothed character 5-gram model ("NGRAM"),[2] in which prediction is conducted by intersecting the history (EEG evidence, plus the wildcard σ) with the LM lattice. In this and our other n-gram models, we used Kneser-Ney smoothing (Kneser and Ney, 1995). The second algorithm we evaluated against was a "prefix language model" that included a character language model (PreLM, Equation 6) explicitly trained on character prefixes of in-vocabulary words (F_{wp})

---

[2] Our choice of an ngram order of 5 was for empirical reasons. A larger window would be too sparse and memory-intensive; a shorter window would not completely capture some of the shorter words that we wanted the model to learn.

combined with a closure over the NGRAM model. This model used an identical prediction mechanism as did the *NGRAM* model, but was designed to be better-equipped to handle in-progress words.

$$PreLM = (F_{NGRAM}\|F_{space})*\|F_{wp} \quad (6)$$

The third is the OCLM described in Section 2. All models were trained on the Brown corpus (Francis and Kučera, 1979), and data split was 80% for training and 20% for testing. The results are on the test set. The test set contained $10,265$ sentences and $176,280$ words. Our simulated task was as follows. For each test sentence, we proceed character by character. At each point in the sentence, we provide the algorithms with some representation of the history of the sentence up to that point, and ask the models to predict the following character target.

We evaluated each model in terms of the traditional average character-level perplexity. Since our model is intended to be used to support character prediction, we also measured the reciprocal rank of the ground-truth target letter, both overall as well as by position within a word (to compare performance earlier in words vs. later). We also looked at the proportion of predictions for which the model placed the correct target letter in the top 10 sorted guesses (ACC@10). We evaluated under two conditions: the first simulating a "deterministic" history, in which we assume that the EEG signal is reliable, and an "ambiguous" history, in which we take the top-n letters from the EEG signal at each time point as possible selections.

3.1 Deterministic History

In this condition, the language model was provided with the "correct" character history up to each prediction point. We refer to this as the $n{=}1$ scenario, as it describes the state of deterministic history of unambiguous and accurate EEG selection at each time point.

Table 1 shows that NGRAM algorithm has subpar performance when compared to both OCLM and PreLM as its Mean Reciprocal Rank (MRR) as well as Perplexity (PPX) are lower and higher respectively. ACC@10 that stands for sentence average prediction for the target within top 10 guesses also demonstrate inferior performance for the NGRAM method.

OCLM and PreLM appear to have similar performance, which surprised us given how different

metric	NGRAM	PreLM	OCLM
MRR	0.4	0.7	0.75
PPX	4.4	1.8	1.9
ACC@10	0.69	0.96	0.96

Table 1: Evaluation Results ($n{=}1$)

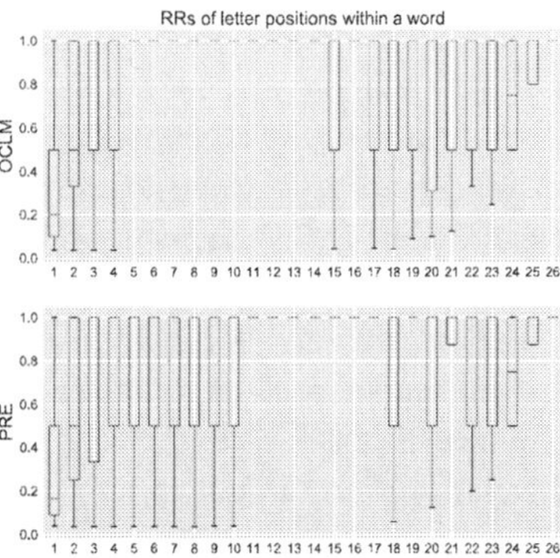

Figure 3: Reciprocal Ranks of letter positions within words ($n{=}1$)

their approaches are. In order to explore more deeply, we attempted to examine the internal behavior within each word in the test set. In Figure 3 the Reciprocal Ranks (RR), are presented for each letter position within a word. The OCLM algorithm demonstrates has higher RR (than PreLM) earlier in the word (position 5 vs. position 11) which is maintained for a longer period of time (10 positions in a row vs 7). Arguably, it is desired that the algorithm would predict correctly as early as possible, as its impact is on greater number of words (there are more words with 5 letters than with 10) and, a longer duration of high RR contributes to more accurate predictions as well. An analogous analysis of perplexity found a similar pattern of *lower* perplexity at *earlier* positions, together with similar duration, and a similar performance profile in OCLM vs PreLM.

3.2 Ambiguous History

Maintaining an ambiguous history of characters for each character selection has the potential to preserve routes the system might have missed otherwise. Erroneous decisions of the system with regards to character predictions unfortunately exist, especially given a noisy channel to process the data from such as the BCI system (different to some degree than typing with a keyboard). In this experiment we examined the performance of OCLM and PreLM with a simulated ambiguous history. We evaluated the OCLM and PreLM algorithms' performance when given histories consisting of the most n likely EEG characters at each time point for $n \in \{2, 3\}$. In all cases, the target character was included, but it was not always the most "probable." Likelihoods were drawn from a Gaussian PDF functions of target and non-target simulating a high performing user [3].

In BCI settings, utterances are often shorter than those that are common in datasets such as the Brown Corpus; therefore, we evaluated on a subset of the test-set containing all sentences of 10 words or less, resulting in $2,954$ sentences with $16,519$ words. For reasons of computational tractability, we simulated an ambiguous history over a window of the immediate past 10 characters; beyond that, we treated history as "fixed," and provided the models with correct targets.[4]

Table 2 presents the results for ambiguous input of n=2 and n=3. Overall adding more history to these type of algorithms degrades their performance. However, the level of degradation seems to vary between OCLM to PreLM. OCLM can produce more accurate predictions and has a higher MRR rate for both ns. PPX also is slightly lower than in PreLM.

nbest	metric	PreLM	OCLM
	MRR	0.29	0.51
n=2	PPX	3.5	3.0
	ACC@10	0.69	0.87
	MRR	0.26	0.44
n=3	PPX	4	3.9
	ACC@10	0.63	0.83

Table 2: Evaluation Results (n=2, n=3)

A further inspection[5] into the letter position performance of n=2 shows that OCLM's MRR remains relatively high (close to 1) especially from the fifth letter position while PreLM falls to values around 0.2. While not shown, the PPX values are consistent again with the MRR behavior. The same pattern appears with a noisier history of n=3. There, OCLM experienced additional degradation, and its high MRR lasted for a shorter term; from the seventh position to the tenth. PreLM's MRR revolved around slightly less than 0.2. OCLM's PPX was relatively low yet higher than of n=2 and was higher for PreLM. This, together with Table 2 indicate a performance

---

[3]The PDFs were overlapping to some degree to enable likelihood confusions of target with non-target

[4]PreLM fails to run on complete ambiguous history

[5]Not included in this work for reasons of space.

degradation in OCLM, but a *break-down* in performance for PreLM. These results emphasize the durability of OCLM over PreLM when the input has more than one possibility.

4 Conclusions

We presented the OCLM architecture for predictive typing with a brain-computer interface. The OCLM enables incorporating ambiguous histories and word-level knowledge to improve its predictions. The OCLM demonstrated improved prediction quality as it takes place earlier in the process and for a longer duration across different conditions of ambiguous input to the system. Our architecture also allows for personalization by employing another lattice to Equation 4 of a user's probable words.

Our future work will focus on integrating the OCLM architecture into our group's BCI system, and evaluating the algorithm with real end-users to see if it reduces the number of sequence displays for each letter selection. Since speed is an important component in the usability of a BCI system, we also plan to assess total typing time as well as accuracy; note that, as our system's predictions become more accurate, the downstream components of our BCI system will also improve.

Another important area of future work will be to more thoroughly investigate our system's handling of OOV words, and identify avenues for improvement as needed. We also hope to take advantage of our model's architecture to provide user-level personalization, and to explore more concrete approaches to autocorrection. Our work to date has focused on the AAC literature, and there is current work in areas such as spelling correction that may prove useful here.

Acknowledgments

We would like to thank the reviewers of the SCLeM workshop for their insightful comments and feedback. We also would like to thank Brian Roark for his helpful advice, as well as our clinical team in the Institute on Development & Disability at OHSU. Research reported in this paper was supported the National Institute on Deafness and Other Communication Disorders of the NIH under award number 5R01DC009834-09. The content is solely the responsibility of the authors and does not necessarily represent the official views of the National Institutes of Health.

References

Cyril Allauzen, Michael Riley, Johan Schalkwyk, Wojciech Skut, and Mehryar Mohri. 2007. OpenFST: A General and Efficient Weighted Finite-State Transducer Library. In *International Conference on Implementation and Application of Automata*, pages 11–23. Springer.

American Speech Language Hearing Association et al. 2004. Roles and Responsibilities of Speech-Language Pathologists with Respect to Augmentative and Alternative Communication: Technical Report.

David R. Beukelman and Pat Mirenda. 2005. *Augmentative & Alternative Communication: Supporting Children & Adults with Complex Communication Needs*, 3rd edition. Paul H. Brookes Publishing Co.

Niels Birbaumer, Nimr Ghanayim, Thilo Hinterberger, Iver Iversen, Boris Kotchoubey, Andrea Kübler, Juri Perelmouter, Edward Taub, and Herta Flor. 1999. A Spelling Device for the Paralysed. *Nature*, 398(6725):297.

Lawrence Ashley Farwell and Emanuel Donchin. 1988. Talking Off the Top of Your Head: Toward a Mental Prosthesis Utilizing Event-Related Brain Potentials. *Electroencephalography and Clinical Neurophysiology*, 70(6):510–523.

Andrew Fowler, Brian Roark, Umut Orhan, Deniz Erdogmus, and Melanie Fried-Oken. 2013. Improved Inference and Autotyping in EEG-Based BCI Typing Systems. In *Proceedings of the 15th International ACM SIGACCESS Conference on Computers and Accessibility*, ASSETS '13, pages 15:1–15:8, New York, NY, USA. ACM.

WN Francis and H Kučera. 1979. Brown Corpus Manual of Information to Accompany a Standard Corpus of Present-Day American English, revised and amplified. *Providence, RI: Brown University, Department of Linguistics*.

Frederick Jelinek. 1997. *Statistical Methods for Speech Recognition*. MIT press.

R. Kneser and H. Ney. 1995. Improved Backing-Off for M-Gram Language Modeling. In *1995 International Conference on Acoustics, Speech, and Signal Processing*, volume 1, pages 181–184 vol.1.

Anderson Mora-Cortes, Nikolay V Manyakov, Nikolay Chumerin, and Marc M Van Hulle. 2014. Language Model Applications to Spelling with Brain-Computer Interfaces. *Sensors*, 14(4):5967–5993.

U. Orhan, K. E. Hild, D. Erdogmus, B. Roark, B. Oken, and M. Fried-Oken. 2012. Rsvp Keyboard: An EEG Based Typing Interface. In *2012 IEEE International Conference on Acoustics, Speech and Signal Processing (ICASSP)*, pages 645–648.

Umut Orhan, Deniz Erdogmus, Brian Roark, Shalini Purwar, Kenneth E Hild, Barry Oken, Hooman Nezamfar, and Melanie Fried-Oken. 2011. Fusion with Language Models Improves Spelling Accuracy for ERP-based Brain Computer Interface spellers. In *Engineering in Medicine and Biology Society, EMBC, 2011 Annual International Conference of the IEEE*, pages 5774–5777. IEEE.

Tom Ouyang, David Rybach, Françoise Beaufays, and Michael Riley. 2017. Mobile Keyboard Input Decoding with Finite-State Transducers. *arXiv preprint arXiv:1704.03987*.

Brian Roark, Richard Sproat, Cyril Allauzen, Michael Riley, Jeffrey Sorensen, and Terry Tai. 2012. The Opengrm Open-Source Finite-State Grammar Software Libraries. In *Proceedings of the ACL 2012 System Demonstrations*, pages 61–66, Jeju Island, Korea. Association for Computational Linguistics.

Eric W Sellers, Theresa M Vaughan, and Jonathan R Wolpaw. 2010. A Brain-Computer Interface for Long-Term Independent Home Use. *Amyotrophic Lateral Sclerosis*, 11(5):449–455.

W Speier, C Arnold, and N Pouratian. 2016. Integrating Language Models into Classifiers for BCI Communication: A Review. *Journal of Neural Engineering*, 13(3):031002.

W Speier, CW Arnold, A Deshpande, J Knall, and N Pouratian. 2015. Incorporating Advanced Language Models into the P300 Speller Using Particle Piltering. *Journal of Neural Engineering*, 12(4):046018.

William Speier, Corey Arnold, Jessica Lu, Ricky K Taira, and Nader Pouratian. 2011. Natural Language Processing with Dynamic Classification Improves P300 Speller Accuracy and Bit Rate. *Journal of Neural Engineering*, 9(1):016004.

Keith Vertanen and Per Ola Kristensson. 2011. The Imagination of Crowds: Conversational AAC Language Modeling Using Crowdsourcing and Large Data Sources. In *Proceedings of the Conference on Empirical Methods in Natural Language Processing*, EMNLP '11, pages 700–711, Stroudsburg, PA, USA. Association for Computational Linguistics.

A. Viterbi. 1967. Error Bounds for Convolutional Codes and an Asymptotically Optimum Decoding Algorithm. *IEEE Transactions on Information Theory*, 13(2):260–269.

Author Index

Adouane, Wafia, 22

Banerjee, Tamali, 55
Bedrick, Steven, 72
Bernardy, Jean-Philippe, 22
Bhattacharyya, Pushpak, 55

Dobnik, Simon, 22
Drozd, Aleksandr, 38
Du, Xiaoyong, 38
Dudy, Shiran, 72
Duh, Kevin, 1

El-Kishky, Ahmed, 12

Ganu, Hrishikesh, 61

Han, Jiawei, 12

Levow, Gina-Anne, 49
Li, Bofang, 38
Liu, Nelson F., 49
Liu, Tao, 38

Macke, Stephen, 12

P, Viswa Datha, 61
Padó, Sebastian, 32
Papay, Sean, 32

Salle, Alexandre, 66
Semmar, Nasredine, 22
Shapiro, Pamela, 1
Smith, David, 72
Smith, Noah A., 49

Villavicencio, Aline, 66
Vu, Ngoc Thang, 32

Xu, Frank, 12
Xu, Shaobin, 72

Zhang, Aston, 12

Association for Computational Linguistics
209 N. Eighth Street
Stroudsburg, Pennsylvania 18360

ISBN 978-1-5108-6361-3